Working Memory and Learning

Working Memory and Learning

A Practical Guide for Teachers

Susan E. Gathercole and
Tracy Packiam Alloway

SAGE Publications
Los Angeles • London • New Delhi • Singapore

SAGE Publications Ltd
1 Oliver's Yard
55 City Road
London
EC1Y 1SP

SAGE Publications Inc
2455 Teller Road
Thousand Oaks, California 91320

SAGE Publications India Pvt Ltd
B1/I1 Mohan Cooperative Industrial Area
Mathura Road, Post Bag 7
New Delhi 110 044

SAGE Publications Asia-Pacific Pte Ltd
33 Pekin Street #02-01
Far East Square
Singapore 048763

Library of Congress Control Number: 2007935892

A catalogue record for this book is available from the British Library

ISBN 978–1-4129–3612-5
ISBN 978–1-4129–3613-2 (pbk)

Typeset by Dorwyn, Wells, Somerset
Printed by Cromwell Press Ltd, Trowbridge, Wiltshire
Printed on paper from sustainable resources

Dedication
For Marcus, Phoebe, Graham, Jess, Stephen, and Jim

Contents

About the authors

Susan E. Gathercole (BSc, PhD, CPsychol) is Professor of Psychology at the University of York, and has held chairs at the universities of Bristol and Durham. She is a cognitive psychologist who specialises in the study of memory and learning in typically-developing children, in children with a variety of developmental disorders, and in adults, and has published over 100 journal articles in these areas. She co-authored an academic book entitled *Working Memory and Language* and has co-edited several other books including *Working Memory in Neuro-developmental Disorders*. Susan is also the co-author of two psychometric tests of memory: the *Working Memory Test Battery for Children* and the *Children's Test of Nonword Repetition*. In recent years, she has been involved in translating basic research into educational practice, in collaboration with academics and professionals from the field of education. She won the British Psychological Society's President's Award for 2007, for her distinguished contribution to psychological understanding.

Tracy Packiam Alloway (PhD) is a senior research psychologist based at the University of Durham. She is interested in how working memory affects learning and has conducted several large-scale studies to find out why children with working memory impairments often fail in classroom activities. Her work has shown that working memory ability predicts later achievement in reading and mathematics. Understanding a child's working memory profile is critical for providing appropriate learning support and she is currently involved in a longitudinal study to develop appropriate intervention for children with memory problems. In addition, she is carrying out several projects to understand how memory affects learning in children with neurodevelopmental disorders such as Attentional Deficit with Hyperactivity Disorder (ADHD), Developmental

Coordination Difficulties (dyspraxia) and dyscalculia (mathematical difficulties).

During the course of her research she has worked with educational professionals, including educational psychologists, learning support coordinators, classroom teachers, and speech and language therapists. In addition to authoring numerous academic articles on how children learn and co-editing a book on developmental disorders, she has developed a computerised screening tool for working memory impairments, Automated Working Memory Assessment, that is being translated into ten languages.

Preface

We are cognitive psychologists whose main interests lie in the basic mental processes that underpin working memory. The simple question that has motivated our work for some time now is: what does working memory do for us in our everyday mental lives? It has become clear that working memory skills are closely associated with learning. Children's abilities to learn in key areas such as reading and mathematics are highly predictable from their scores on working memory tests: individuals who are making slow progress in these areas typically score very poorly on these measures.

These links between working memory and learning ability in childhood seem to us to be important not only for cognitive theory, but also for educational practice. With this in mind, we embarked several years ago on a mission to share our findings with professional groups such as teachers, educational (school) psychologists, and speech and language therapists to whom we thought they were relevant. The research findings were presented to these groups and they usually seemed to be interested. After our presentations, members of the audience almost always asked the same two important questions: what problems do these children face in the classroom, and what can we do to help them? Unfortunately, we were not able at that time to provide proper answers. The reason that our research, like that of the rest of the field, involved testing large numbers of children (hundreds, in some cases) on a variety of measures that tapped working memory, reading, mathematics and other abilities. Some time later, we would score the child's performance on the various measures we had administered, enter the data into a statistical package, and perform analyses on the data. So at the point at which we tested an individual child, we simply did not know whether he or she had poor working memory or was making slow academic progress. Neither did we have any idea about the particular day-to-day difficulties that children with poor working memory were encountering in the classroom, or the consequences of these for their behaviour. And without knowing this, we couldn't even hazard a guess about how to help such children overcome their learning difficulties.

Here we learned an important lesson about translating research into practice within the field of education. This is that the child is central, and that it is necessary to understand what is happening (or not happening) for the individual child if we are to get any useful grasp on why learning is not proceeding smoothly and on ways that learning can be effectively supported. Pointing to research findings that establish particular associations with learning – in this case, relating to working memory – is simply not enough. To be relevant to educational practice, the research needs to address directly fundamental questions about what is happening for the child.

Guided by this insight, we have changed the way that we conduct much of our research. Many of the methods that we now employ are a far cry from laboratory-based cognitive psychology paradigms. Our first activity involved spending several months observing children with poor working memory – in the course of their daily classroom lives. We are hugely grateful to Emily Lamont for her sterling work in unobtrusively watching and meticulously recording what happened for these children in the classroom. She documented the frustrations, failures and missed learning opportunities that we now know characterise children with poor working memory when the ongoing activity imposes a heavy burden of working memory. These observations and the insights that they brought have provided the foundations for our subsequent work. This has involved identifying the classroom behaviour of children with poor working memory, and developing a classroom-based approach designed to prevent the working memory overload that we believe is the cause of the slow academic progress of the children.

Observation remains the touchstone of our work in this field, and we have depended heavily on this method both to help us understand and evaluate how the intervention can work in practice and to identify good practice that can be disseminated. Hannah Kirkwood, an experienced teacher who we are extremely fortunate to have in our research team, has done a fantastic job of observing children with poor working memory both in regular classrooms and in classrooms implementing the intervention. The observation notes and case studies in this book that illustrate how working memory relates to learning for the individual child are entirely hers, and we owe her a huge debt of gratitude for recording and reporting this material.

Engaging with the children at this more personal level has influenced our thinking and our goals in many ways. We have been particularly troubled by the ways in which failures of working memory so often go undetected in the classroom, or are (what seem to us) misclassified as failures of attention (such as 'not listening' or being 'easily distracted') or of motivation ('just not interested'). This simply does not fit with our own experiences of children with poor working memory. What we usually see is a child who starts a task well but then forgets the crucial information needed to guide an activity; if no help is at hand, they may well then become distracted or start to daydream. Intervening at the right point can help keep the child on task. So, one of the points on our agenda is to persuade those who are responsible for guiding a child's learning to bear in mind that these kinds of behaviour may be direct consequences of working memory failures, and that they can be at least minimised by effective classroom management.

Our classroom experiences have also led us to believe that children with poor working memory are important in their own right, and that they require special support as they struggle to meet the regular demands of the classroom. In research on developmental disorders of learning, it is much more common for working memory problems to be considered as one of several secondary characteristics of disorders including dyslexia, language impairment, or ADHD. In none of these cases do the diagnostic criteria for the disorders include working memory impairments, although the majority of children in each case do have problems in this area. It seems to us to be timely now to step back and consider whether children with poor working memory merit recognition either on this basis alone, or on its co-occurrence with significant academic learning difficulties. Poor working memory is certainly as prevalent as the disorders mentioned above: we typically work with the 10% of children with the lowest working memory scores for their age group and, as we report in Chapter 4, the great majority of these children struggle with learning.

Another concern we have is that the relevant research literature on working memory problems in developmental disorders has become unduly preoccupied by the debate about whether or not these problems are core deficits or are simply secondary consequences of other more basic problems. While this debate may be of considerable theoretical importance, it may not be very relevant to the practicalities of classroom learning. For the record, we believe that whereas some children have a core working memory deficit, in other individuals with problems in areas such as language or coordination the working memory deficits are probably secondary. But at a practical level, it probably matters only whether children are or are not able to meet the working memory demands of a particular learning activity. If they are not, they will need support if they are to succeed and to learn, irrespective of the cause of their low working memory capacity. It is therefore not necessary to differentiate the kind of support that is provided for the child on the basis of whether poor working memory is a core deficit or a consequence of another basic disorder. In practical terms, it is probably more useful to know where a child's strengths as well as weaknesses lie, and to use this information to identify the strategies and other kinds of environmental support likely to benefit the individual child. This too is an important theme of the book.

Another lesson we have learned from our attempts to translate research into educational practice is the importance of working closely with teachers and other professional groups who engage on a daily level with the practicalities of helping children learn and to take advantage of the skills and experience that they bring to bear. Our thinking has been enriched by the many practitioners who have shared with us their ideas about their own pupils with working memory problems, and who have furnished us the many examples of excellent practice that we present in the later chapters of the book.

Finally, we thank our families for their support while this book was being prepared. Martin and Ross generously tolerated the many absences of body and mind with which it was associated, and never failed to give us encouragement when it was needed. We must also mention our children, without whom the book might well have been easier to write but our lives would not have been half as much fun. This book is dedicated to them, with our love.

CHAPTER 1

An introduction to working memory

Overview

This chapter provides an introduction to working memory and how it is used in everyday life. It describes the limits of working memory, the causes of loss of information from working memory, and how the components of working memory function. Differences between working memory and other kinds of memory are discussed, and the characteristics of different kinds of long-term memory are outlined.

Introduction

When asked recently to describe what working memory is, a group of teachers working with young children made the following comments.

'No idea. Never heard of it.'
'I don't know, but I have a terrible memory. I can never remember children's names, telephone numbers or other pieces of information.'
'Is it similar to short-term and long-term memory?'

You may be similarly uncertain about what working memory is, and what impact it has on how children function in the classroom. The purpose of this chapter is to answer some of the questions that are often asked about working memory, and to explain how it works. By the end of this chapter, you should be familiar with what working memory is and have a reasonable understanding of its everyday uses. You will also learn how working memory differs from other kinds of memory that retain information for much longer periods of time – hours, days, years and, in some cases, decades. Working memory, in contrast, is useful only for remembering a small amount of information for a matter or seconds, or minutes at most.

What is working memory?

'Working memory' is the term used by psychologists to refer to the ability we have to hold and manipulate information in the mind over short periods of time. It provides a mental workspace or jotting pad that is used to store important information in the course of our everyday lives.

One example of an activity that uses working memory is mental arithmetic. Imagine, for example, that you are attempting to multiply together the numbers 43 and 67 in a situation where you are unable to use either a calculator or a pen and paper. To do this, you would first need to store the two numbers in working memory. The next step would be to use the multiplication rules you have already learned to calculate the products of successive pairs of numbers, adding to working memory the products as you go. Finally, you would need to add together the products held in working memory, arriving at a final solution.

This process imposes quite considerable burdens of working memory: several number combinations need to be kept in working memory for the amount of time it takes to make these calculations, and the contents of working memory have to be updated to include our number calculations as we proceed through the stages of the calculation. Without working memory, it would not be possible to carry out this kind of complex mental activity without having some means to make an external record of the numbers and the calculations.

We usually experience mental activities that place significant demands on working memory as a kind of mental juggling in which we try to keep all elements of the task – in the case of mental arithmetic, the original numbers we are trying to multiply as well as the calculations we make as we proceed – going at the same time. Often, the juggling attempt will fail, either because the capacity of working memory is exceeded, or because we become distracted and our attention is diverted away from the task in hand. A minor distraction such as an unrelated thought springing to mind or an interruption by someone else is likely to result in complete loss of the stored information, and so in a failed calculation attempt. As no amount of effort will allow us to remember again the lost information, the only course of action is to start the calculation afresh.

Here are some more examples of everyday activities that depend on working memory.

- Following directions such as 'When you pass the church on the left, turn immediately right and then take the second left.'
- Hearing an unfamiliar word in a foreign language and attempting to repeat it several seconds later.
- Adding up and remembering the total amount spent as you select items from shelves at the supermarket and add them to your basket.
- Remembering to measure and combine the correct amounts of ingredients ('rub in 50g of margarine and 100g of flour, then add 75g of sugar'), when the recipe is no longer in view.

Is there a limit to what working memory can hold?

Yes, the amount of information that can be held in working memory for even a short period of time is strictly limited and if this limit is exceeded, we will forget at least some of what we are trying to remember. For example, multiplying larger numbers such as 542 and 891 'in our heads' is for most of us out of the question, even though it does not require greater mathematical knowledge than calculating the product of a pair of two-digit numbers. The reason we cannot do this is simply because it would require the storage of more information than the limited capacity of working memory can hold.

It is often said that the average adult cannot hold more than six or seven units of information in working memory. This is the upper limit, and for some kinds of information such as meaningless patterns the amount we can store in working memory is much less. You will notice that the capacity of working memory is described here in terms of units of information: so, what exactly is a unit? The answer depends on whether the material to be remembered is organised in a meaningful way, or not. A digit in a sequence that comprises a telephone or a PIN number or a single item in a shopping list, all represent single units. However, if the individual elements can be grouped together in a larger chunk, then this chunk becomes a unit. For example, it is difficult to remember nine letters that do not form a spelling pattern such as *JDIWMXLPQ*, but if we are able to group a sequence of letters of the same length into meaningful units such as *BBC-IBM-USA*, then remembering nine letters is less of a problem. Similarly, most adults can just about remember a list of about six words such as *hat, walk, roof, duck, tree,* and *banana* that are not related to one another in meaning. If, however, the sequence of words forms a meaningful sentence such as *When the man walked down the street he saw a red fox crossing the road* which consists of more than twice as many words, it is quite easy to remember. In this case, memory for the sentence can be supported not only by working memory, but also by our memory for the meaning of the sentence. Combining these two sources of memory – working memory, and memory for meaning – boosts memory performance dramatically.

Another factor that influences how well a particular piece of information is remembered is its location within a larger sequence of material. Consider attempting to remember a list of words such as *hat, walk, roof, duck, tree, banana, car* and *sun*, in this order. Because the list contains eight words (that is, eight units because the material cannot easily be chunked), it is likely to exceed the working memory capacity of most people, resulting in errors. Interestingly, it is quite predictable where the errors are likely to occur: we are most likely to forget items from the middle of the list. Recall of the items at the very beginning of lists is relatively good because we have had more opportunity to rehearse these, and rehearsal boosts recall. This advantage to items at the beginning of a list is known as the primacy effect. Recall is also very accurate for the final items in a sequence, and this is known as the recency effect. It occurs mainly because we do not have to hold the material in working memory for as long. Recall of the final item in a list is particularly accurate if it has been spoken rather than just read – it sometimes seems as though you can hear an echo of the most recent word that has been uttered, and this lingers on for several seconds. As a result, it can be useful to say something aloud rather than reading it silently if you want to recall it a brief time later.

The sound patterns of the words that we are trying to remember can also have an impact on the accuracy with which they are held in working memory. Sequences of words that are distinct such as *bus, clock, spoon, fish* and *mouse* are much easier to remember than a list of words that sound very similar such as *man, cat, map, mat, can* and *cap*, because we are much less likely to confuse their sounds in working memory.

How much information can be stored in working memory is also affected by background noise. The contents of working memory are best preserved in silence, and are strongly disrupted by hearing speech that is unrelated – this might consist of a conversation by other people in the same room, or may come from the television or radio. It is almost impossible to prevent this kind of material from disrupting the contents of working memory, leading to greater rates of forgetting than in quiet conditions. Constant background noise that does not involve language, such as the hum of a vacuum cleaner or the sound of a lawn mower, has little discernible effect. You may, however, be startled when a noise starts, and this could distract you from attending to the contents of working memory which may then cause accelerated loss of information.

Most of us employ strategies to prolong the period over which information is stored in working memory, even if we are not consciously aware of doing so. One common strategy is to rehearse the contents of working memory; often, this takes the form of repeatedly saying 'in our heads' the material to be remembered, until the point at which the information can be used. So, if we are told a new telephone number that we want to dial when we go to the next room to find the phone, it is likely that we will repeat the sequence either silently, in a whisper or out loud, to keep it in mind. One factor that influences the effectiveness of rehearsal in maintaining the contents of working memory is the length of the material being rehearsed. Words that take longer to pronounce, such as *refrigerator*, *hippopotamus, Mississippi*, and *aluminium*, take longer to rehearse and so are less easily maintained than short words such as *bus, clock, spoon* and *fish*.

Being aware of your memory strengths and limitations can enable you to deploy compensatory strategies very effectively. When one of the authors was discussing rehearsal recently with a group of teachers, a member of the audience described how both she and her husband had evolved a strategy of sharing their working memory resources when necessary. When they were given lengthy telephone numbers to remember, they would try to remember half of the sequence each, and so combine their working memory capacities. They also were aware that although rehearsing their part of the sequence helped, hearing the other person rehearse aloud was very disruptive, and this led to them establishing a 'silent rehearsal only' agreement that would min-imise mutual interference and distraction. By being aware of their own personal limits in this way, this couple were able to increase their individual working memory capacities.

Although rehearsal can be extremely useful in these situations, there are other kinds of mental activities that involve working memory for which it is much less appropriate. Mental arithmetic is a good example of this. It involves retrieving our knowledge of number rules and apply-ing this knowledge, as well as storing the numbers to be operated on and any interim numbers already generated, and rehearsing the num-bers has the unfortunate consequence of disturbing the mental activity of making the calculations. Rehearsal is therefore a strategy that is most effective when the current activity involves only storage, as in the case of remembering a new telephone number. When it is necessary to engage in other demanding mental activities as well as storing informa-tion in working memory, rehearsal is much less useful.

Other strategies that people develop across time to cope with the limits to working memory are often idiosyncratic, and play to their individual mental strengths. For example, some people have extremely good abilities to generate mental images of information and of remembering these for quite long periods of time. Instead of writing down a shopping list, these individuals may imagine and remember a route through their local supermarket in which they stop at particular locations in the aisles at which they can retrieve each item. This uses long-term memory, so that they will be able to recollect the route several hours later when they arrive in the supermarket, rather than short-term memory. Other people have from an early age remarkable abilities to remember information such as numbers in terms of colours or other sensations that they strongly associate them with (an ability known as synaesthesia), and this for them provides a highly effective way of remembering. However, most of us cannot do this.

Sometimes we hear of individuals who have exceptional abilities to remember huge amounts of meaningless information, and may indeed have made a career on this basis. For example, cases have been reported of people who can remember sequences of more than 100 digits in their original sequence. Do they have working memory capacities that are ten times or more greater than our own? Rather surprisingly, it appears not. What distinguishes such individuals from the rest of us is that they have developed and practised highly systematic and elaborate strategies that support their memory without relying on the rather limited working memory system. For example, one mnemonist was also an accomplished athlete, and would remember runs of numbers within the larger sequence in terms of the fastest times for races of various distances over famous routes. This is a good example of the use of chunking, described in an earlier section, as a way of decreasing working memory load and exploiting knowledge that has already been learned and organised into chunks. In situations in which their highly developed strategies are not appropriate, mnemonists typically show evidence of good but by no means exceptional working memory capacities. It is therefore clear that their undoubted memory strengths come from the strategies they have developed that exploit existing knowledge, reducing the dependence on working memory.

Does working memory capacity vary between people?

Yes, there is a personal limit to working memory, with each individual having a relatively fixed capacity that may be greater or lesser than that of others. This capacity is largely consistent over different occasions, although the other factors affecting working memory that were discussed in the section above will influence memory accuracy on particular occasions. Because of the substantial variation in working memory capacity found between individuals, it is necessary when interacting with others to bear in mind that their working memory capacities may not be the same as ours, and for this reason we may have to modify how we pass on information to them – how much information, and at what rate. As we will see later in the book, this is an important consideration for an adult working with young children, as their working memories are even more limited in capacity than those of older children and adults.

What causes information to be lost from working memory?

Because working memory capacity is limited, it can easily fail us. Typically, information in working memory is lost very quickly, within a few seconds. The contents can be lost either because our attention is distracted from it so that it fades very rapidly, or it is displaced by other information. The loss of information from working memory can to some extent be prevented by maintaining attention on it, an experience that literally feels like holding something in mind. Here are some of the situations that lead to the loss of the contents of working memory.

- *Distraction.* An unrelated thought springing to mind, an interruption by someone else, or another distraction within the environment such as a telephone ringing or a child crying is often sufficient to cause information to be lost from working memory. This is because unless we continue to attend to the contents of working memory, the stored information decays very rapidly and is soon lost for good. It is therefore very important to minimise likely distractions if we are going to make effective use of working memory.

- *Doing something else at the same time.* Activities that require attention to be switched to another effortful activity are disruptive because they divert attention from the information being stored in working memory, leading to accelerated loss of information. These attention-demanding processes may be an intrinsic part of our ongoing activity, as in the case of using our stored mathematical knowledge when engaged in mental arithmetic. In these situations, the diversion of attention from the stored contents of working memory (the digits, and the calculations made so far) is inevitable. However, it is beneficial to switch attention from the processing (mental calculation) to the items being stored as rapidly and frequently as possible, as engaging in lengthy processing without mentally re-checking the contents of working memory will lead to rapid decay.

What happens to information when it is lost from working memory?

Once information has been lost from working memory, it cannot be recovered. In this situation, the only option is to start again. Consider again the mental arithmetic problem given in the beginning of this chapter: *43 x 67*. If we had calculated *43 x 7 = 301*, and began calculating *43 x 60*, but then forgot our response to *43 x 7*, the sum would have to be re-calculated from the beginning. We are not able to retrieve the numbers that we had produced by simply trying to 'think back' on what we did, as the memory traces are no longer there. In this way, forgetting information in working memory is very different from forgetting, for example, where you parked your car, or whether or not you brought that important document in to work. In these cases, you can try to retrieve the information by mentally retracing your steps and stand a good chance of remembering the critical information. When you forget information in working memory, you are not able to do this. This could explain why a child may stare blankly at the teacher when asked what he or she intends to do next. Asking them to *Try to remember what I said to you* is unlikely to help, as the crucial information will probably have been completely lost from their working memory.

How does working memory work?

Working memory is actually a system of inter-linked memory components that are located in different parts of the brain. Some of these components are specialised to store material of particular kinds; these are often referred to as short-term memory, although they are part of the larger working memory system. Verbal short-term memory stores material that can be expressed in spoken language, such as numbers, words and sentences, and is supported by structures in the side part of the left hemisphere of the brain. We know this because individuals who have experienced injury to these parts of the brain lose their abilities to remember verbal material for short periods of time, and also because the blood flow to these areas increases when a person tries to remember verbal material. The process of rehearsal described earlier in the chapter is an important part of verbal short-term memory.

Visuo-spatial short-term memory can hold images, pictures and information about locations. If we studied a picture and then had to recall the physical characteristics and locations of the objects it con-tained when the picture was no longer in view, we would need to rely on visuo-spatial short-term memory. This part of working memory is located in the right hemisphere, the opposite side of the brain from verbal short-term memory, and is a completely different system. Because verbal and visuo-spatial short-term memory are separate, a person who is very good at storing verbal material will not necessarily have excellent visuo-spatial storage abilities, and *vice versa*.

The final part of working memory is a more general component that controls attention and is involved in higher-level mental processes, and is often called the 'central executive'. This is a very important component because it is involved in all mental activities that involve coordinating both storage and effortful mental processing, such as mental arithmetic and many classroom activities, as described more fully in later chapters. These activities will depend both on the central executive and either one or both of the short-term memory components (verbal and visuo-spatial), according to the nature of the activity. Mental arithmetic, for example, will involve both the central executive and verbal short-term memory. In other activities, the central executive and visuo-spatial short-term memory may work in combination. Unlike the two short-term memory components, the central executive is located in the front regions of both the left and right hemispheres of the brain.

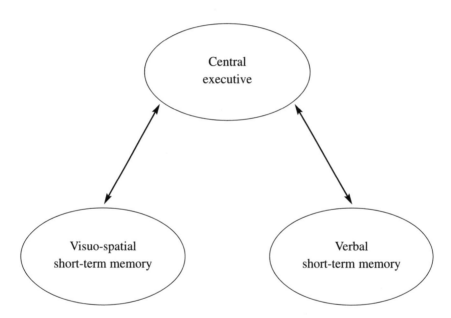

Figure 1.1 *A model summarising the main components of working memory*

The three main components of working memory are shown in Figure 1.1. Although it is simple, this diagram (which cognitive psychologists call a 'model') is based on evidence from many experiments on working memory, and also from studies that have investigated the activity of the brain when people are involved in mental activities that engage working memory. A few features of this model are particularly important to note. First, each of the components has its own limited capacity. Second, there are links running in both directions between the two short-term memory stores and the central executive. This means that the pairs of components can work directly together and exchange information as appropriate. Third, there is no corresponding path between visuo-spatial and verbal short-term memory. Because these two components store information in fundamentally different forms that are not compatible with one another, they cannot communicate directly, although they can be indirectly linked through the central executive. Finally, unlike the short-term memory stores, the central executive provides cognitive resources related to attention that can be allocated to material in any possible format. One practical consequence of this is that an individual who has low central executive capacity will typically encounter more difficulties in working memory activities that place demands on the central executive, irrespective of the particular format of information that is being handled.

Working memory as a whole consists of the combination of these three components, and any particular activity might engage some or all of them. There is a large research literature devoted to investigating in detail how each of these components work in both children and adults. For the purposes of this book, it is mostly sufficient to distinguish between two main terms – working memory and short-term memory.

How is short-term memory different from working memory?

From reading the previous section, you may already understand that the two short-term memory components (verbal and visuo-spatial short-term memory) form part but not the whole of the larger working memory system. Psychologists use the term 'short-term memory' to refer to those situations in which the individual simply has to store some material without either manipulating it mentally in some way, or doing something else at the same time. Remembering a telephone number is a good example of an activity that depends on short-term memory – in this case, verbal short-term memory. Working memory is an umbrella term for the larger system of which short-term memory is a part, and activities that tax the central executive (possibly in combination with the short-term memory stores) are often described as working memory tasks. In practice, these tend to be more complex activities than short-term memory tasks, involving not only the storage of information, but also either its mental transformation or being engaged in some other effortful mental process. The distinction between the meaning of the terms 'short-term memory' and 'working memory' is important to understand because they play different roles in learning new skills, particularly during childhood. More information on the precise links between short-term memory, working memory and learning is provided in Chapter 3.

One source of confusion arises because the phrase 'short-term memory' has now entered everyday language, and is widely used to mean something rather different to the psychologists' definition. Informally, the term is often used to refer to the relatively recent past, such as something that happened earlier in the same day or possibly the previous day. In fact, the contents of working memory (or the short-term memory stores that it encompasses) could not extend over this lengthy period, and indeed usually last for no more than seconds. The type of memory to which this everyday use of short-term memory refers is what psychologists call 'episodic memory', and is classified as a long-term rather than short-term memory system because the information it retains can survive lengthy delays and distraction. Episodic memory is a very important aspect of memory that underpins our recollection of events or episodes that occurred relatively recently. In the following section, information about this and other kinds of long-term memory is provided.

Long-term memory?

The term 'long-term memory' is reserved for memory of experiences that occurred at a point in time prior to the immediate past or near present, and also for knowledge that has been acquired over long periods of time. There are several different kinds of long-term memory, each with its own unique psychological properties. The characteristics of the four main kinds of long-term memory are briefly described below, and are summarised in Table 1.1.

Episodic memory

This part of long-term memory stores memories for specific events in the relatively recent past – events that occurred either minutes, hours or days ago. Episodic memory is used to remember the mundane details of life, such as what you had for breakfast this morning, where you parked the car when you arrived at work and, possibly, what clothes you were wearing yesterday. Although episodic memory can retain many details of events, it is certainly not a perfect record of our experiences that resembles a video recording or an audio tape. Rather, episodic memory stores our mental interpretation of our experiences, and tends to be best at retaining the most important or notable features of events. These memories fade rapidly unless they are later retrieved, rehearsed or discussed and, in practice, we are unlikely to remember any of the details of relatively routine aspects of our lives after a small number of days. So, it is unlikely that we will remember what we wore to work a week ago, although it is relatively easy to recall what we wore yesterday. We may, however, remember for a much longer period a surprise encounter with an old friend, or the time that we unexpectedly received some shocking news. This is in part because such non-routine events are often reflected upon and discussed subsequently, which can both prolong their retention in episodic memory and also lead to the event being stored in a more permanent system – autobiographical memory, that is described next.

Autobiographical memory

Some information about our lives is retained in an even longer lasting memory system known as 'autobiographical memory'. Autobiographical memory stores two main kinds of information. One is the set of our personal facts including our name, information about family and friends, and the nature of our major lifetime periods such as what schools we attended, what jobs we have had, what houses we lived in. Autobiographical memory also retains memory of significant and sometimes emotionally charged experiences from our life. Some of these memories are quite predictable, such as the first day at school or nursery, birth of siblings, wedding days, and birth of children. Other personal memories are much more idiosyncratic, and we may not know why we remember this event in particular. Typically, the earliest distinct memory that can be remembered dates back to about three or four years of age.

Semantic memory

The stored knowledge that we have acquired about the world through our personal experiences is held in semantic memory. One important part of semantic memory is our mental lexicon of language, which stores information about words such as their meaning, their pronunciation and their spelling. Semantic memory links together the words in our mental lexicon, so that we know how different concepts are related to one another. For example, we know that a dog is a mammal and that mammals are animals, and that Paris is the capital of France. We also know that although bread and butter are distinct concepts, they are closely associated with each other. Semantic memory also retains detailed knowledge of the visual characteristics of concrete objects, and of other familiar entities such as the faces of people that we can recognise. When we encounter an event that corresponds to an item stored in semantic memory – such as when we read the word *dog* – it also activates to some extent related concepts such as *cat, lead,* and *kennel.* In this way, it is easier to recognise something – whether it is a word or a physical object – that is related to something else we have experienced very recently. So, our recent experiences interact with knowledge about the world that is stored permanently in semantic memory. A feature of semantic memory that distinguishes it from episodic memory is that we are unable to recall the time when we learnt the facts that are stored in it, probably because we have repeatedly encountered the fact so many times: we simply 'know' them. In contrast, episodic memories are located very specifically in a particular place and time, and so we describe ourselves as 'remembering' rather than 'knowing' them.

Procedural memory

Actions or skills that we have learnt through practice and now have become automatic form part of a very basic long-term memory system known as procedural memory. A hallmark of procedural memory is that although we know that we can do something, we cannot describe easily the precise ways in which we can do it. Good examples of such skills are walking, whistling, riding a bicycle or driving a car. Procedural memory is one of the most basic forms of memory, and is probably not exclusive to the human species. This kind of memory is also very stable, tends to persist over many decades, and is fairly resistant to disruption by disease or old age.

Working memory and long-term memory can work together

There are many kinds of remembering that do not rely on working memory. Without working memory, we can get on a bike and cycle it successfully, understand the meaning of a printed sentence and say it out loud, recall an event from our childhood, and remember who we went out to dinner with last night and what we ate. In each case, these feats of memory involve long-term rather than working memory. This does not mean that these kinds of memory are irrelevant to situations in which we are trying to remember information for a brief period of time. Although working memory is distinct from long-term memory, material that is stored in long-term memory can boost our immediate memory performance by decreasing reliance on the very limited capacity of working memory. We are therefore more likely to remember a string or list of words that are meaningful to us, such as the name of our favourite foods or of ingredients in a highly familiar recipe, than a random combination of words that we have not previously encountered. The memory benefit does not arise because our working memory capacity has changed in any way, but instead because we can use other sources of memory information that can be used to bolster the fragile working memory system. As we will see in later chapters, using long-term memory to supplement working memory is an excellent strategy for increasing our chances of meeting the memory demands of many activities.

Table 1.1 Characteristics of different kinds of memories

Kind of memory	Duration	Type of information	Example
Short-term	Seconds	Verbal or non-verbal	Briefly remembering an unfamiliar phone number
Working	Seconds	Any kind	Following lengthy directions of how to reach a location
Episodic	Hours to days	Details of particular experiences	Remembering what you had for breakfast this morning
Autobiographical	Lifetime	Basic facts and conceptual knowledge	Remembering your wedding day
Semantic	Lifetime, with regular exposure	Knowledge, including personal facts	Knowing that Paris is the capital of France
Procedural	Lifetime once skill is established	Any kind of skill that can be used automatically	Knowing how to drive a car

POINTS TO REMEMBER

- Working memory is used to hold information in mind and manipulate it for brief periods of time.

- Working memory is limited in capacity. The capacity varies between individuals and is affected by characteristics of the material that is being stored.

- Information is lost from working memory when we are distracted, or its limited capacity is overloaded.

- Working memory is a system of linked components, consisting of short-term memory stores for verbal (language) and visual or spatial information, and a coordinating component that controls attention that is called the central executive.

- Short-term memory involves storage, whereas working memory is involved more generally when a task involves storing and mentally manipulating information.

- There are four main kinds of long-term memory: episodic memory, autobiographical memory, semantic memory and procedural memory.

CHAPTER 2

Working memory in childhood

Overview

This chapter describes the changes that take place in working memory over the course of childhood, and also the substantial differences in working memory capacity that exist between children of the same age. Methods for assessing the strengths and weaknesses in working memory that are convenient for use in the classroom and for helping identify strategies for learning support are outlined. Finally, differences and similarities between working memory and intelligence, or IQ, are discussed.

Introduction

Here is a sequence of numbers. Study it, cover with your hand, and then try to remember them in the same order.

3 9 5 4 7

Next, attempt to remember this longer sequence.

1 7 6 3 9 5 8

Now try something different. Study the list below, and then attempt to recall the sequence in reverse order, starting with the last number and ending with the first one.

8 3 9 2 7

Finally, try to remember this sequence, again in reverse order.

4 1 7 6 3 9 2

If you managed to resist the temptation to look at those numbers more than once before you recalled them, you would probably have discovered that the longer sequences were harder to remember, although you may still have been just about able to correctly recall the seven-digit list in forwards order. Recalling lists in backward order would have been much more difficult, and you are likely to have made errors for the longer list. Forward and backward digit recall are two measures that are commonly used to measure the capacity of working memory. In these tests, the first lists that are presented consist only of two items, and then are gradually increased in length until errors are made, at which point testing is stopped. The length at which an individual can remember a sequence at about 50% accuracy is known as memory span, and reflects his or her personal memory limits on a particular task. On average, forward digit span for an adult is around seven items, and backward digit span is either four or five.

Forward digit span provides a measure of verbal short-term memory: it only requires the rememberer to store and faithfully reproduce the material, without the need to mentally transform it. Backward digit recall, on the other hand, involves not only remembering but also reversing the sequence in which the numbers were presented, which is a challenging mental activity. Because this task combines short-term memory and other significant mental processing, backward digit span draws upon both verbal short-term memory and the central executive components of working memory. As such, it therefore provides a measure of working memory rather than of short-term memory.

The capacity of working memory increases across the childhood years. This is illustrated in Figure 2.1 which shows the performance of typical children aged from 5 to 15 years on tests of the three main aspects of working memory: verbal short-term memory, visuo-spatial short-term memory, and working memory (which involves the central executive and at least one of the short-term memory components). The scale of the graph is not important: a score of 100 on the y axis simply corresponds to average performance across all groups from ages 4 to 15. The growth functions are very similar for all three aspects of working memory, with marked working memory capacity between

5 and 11 years of age, followed by small but significant increases up to 15 years when adult levels are reached. Typically, the memory spans of adults are between two and three times greater than those of young children. So, the longest sequence of numbers that a typical four-year-old child would be expected to remember in backwards sequence is two (for example, *8 3*). In contrast, the average 15-year-old would stand a good chance of correctly recalling in reverse sequence a four-digit list such as *8 3 9 2*, and possibly also a five-digit sequence.

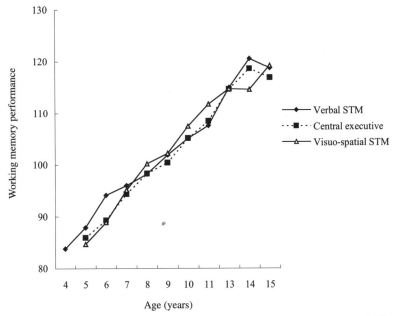

Figure 2.1 *The development of the different components of working memory in childhood*

Not all children of the same age have the same working memory capacities. In fact, as shown in Figure 2.2, differences between individual children can be very large indeed. Look first at the average levels of performance for children of different ages, denoted by the squares located mid-way between the horizontal bars in each case. These values gradually increase with age, as we would expect, with a typical seven-year-old having a slightly greater working memory capacity than that of a typical six-year-old, and slightly less than that of a typical eight-year-old. The horizontal bars extending upwards and downwards from these mid-points reflect the 90th and 10th centile points for each age group. This means that the top end point of the bar corresponds to the score of a child who is in the top 10% for his or her age group, and the bottom end of the bar to the score of a child who is in the bottom 10%. In a class of 30 children who represent the typical range of abilities for their age, there will therefore be three pupils scoring at or above the 90th centile point, and a further three pupils with scores at or below the 10th centile level.

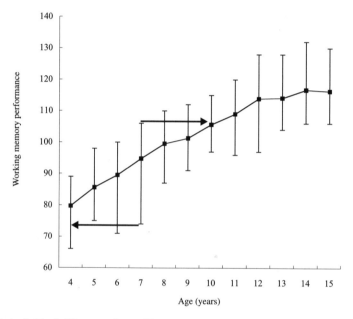

Figure 2.2 *Individual differences in working memory capacity in childhood. The top points of the horizontal bars correspond to the 90th centile, and the bottom points to the 10th centile. The left and right arrows are discussed in the text.*

Now take a look at the 10th centile point (shown by the left arrow ←) for the seven-year-old age group, which represents a child with poor working memory capacity. If you track this point along to the left, to the point at which it intersects with the solid line reflecting age-appropriate working memory capacity, you will see that this level of performance is even less than that of an average four-year-old child. This can be contrasted with a seven-year-old child at the 90th centile (represented by the right arrow →), who has a score corresponding to that of an average ten-year-old child. This means that it would be reasonable to expect a six-year range in working memory capacity to be represented within a typical class of seven-year-old children. We will see later in this chapter that this magnitude of difference in the working memory capacities of individual children has a very direct impact on the extent to which they can meet the working memory demands of classroom learning activities.

Developmental changes in working memory

In this section, some of the most important changes in the different aspects of working memory and other associated cognitive abilities during childhood are described.

Working memory

In Chapter 1, a model of working memory was described that consisted of three components: the central executive, verbal short-term memory and visuo-spatial short-term memory. Working memory capacity is measured by tasks that involve some effortful mental processing, which are supported by the central executive and at least one of the two short-term stores. For example, both the central executive and verbal short-term memory contribute to backward digit span performance.

One of the reasons that working memory capacity increases as children grow older is that they become more efficient at carrying out mental processes. We know that this is the case because if performance on a particular task – such as counting the number of objects in a display – is directly measured, then, on average, older children perform faster than younger children. The improvement in counting efficiency occurs even beyond the age at which the children have completely mastered counting, and so is not simply due to the fact that some of the children in the age groups do not have the knowledge to perform the task. Similarly, the speed with which children can name aloud a familiar printed word such as *dog* becomes faster as the children get older, even though the children may accurately name the correct word at all ages. What is happening here is that the mental processes involved in these skills – counting and reading – are becoming faster and more efficient with increasing experience. By 14 or 15 years, processing efficiency reaches adult levels.

The increases in working memory capacity that occur as children grow older are partly a result of these increases in the efficiency of processing. It has been suggested that every individual has a single, limited pool of mental resources that support working memory, and that these resources are used both to store material and to carry out processing activities, such as counting and reading. Working memory activities that involve difficult processing will therefore leave fewer resources to support memory storage than those that involve easy or no processing. Consistent with this view, research has shown that memory performance typically declines as the difficulty of the processing element of a working memory activity increases. This same logic provides a simple explanation for the growth of working memory capacity during childhood: because processing efficiency increases, there are more resources available for memory storage, leading to superior memory performance.

This theory also explains some of the difficulties encountered by children in working memory tasks. Consider the following instruction given by a teacher.

> Listen to these numbers, work out the pattern, and then tell me which ones should be where the blanks are: 0, 3, 6, blank, 12, blank, 18.

If the child has either not learned the three-times-table or is not highly practised at using it, it will take him or her a relatively long time to identify each of the missing numbers as it will not be possible to use a mental 'look-up' table. Instead, the child will have to engage in other more time-consuming strategies, such as identifying units of three, either by counting aloud or by using fingers. Because of the high processing demands of these strategies, the child is likely to forget the original sequence spoken by the teacher, and may also forget a missing number that he or she did manage to identify (such as 9 in the example given above). In this way, increases in processing demands are accompanied by reductions in the working memory storage that is available.

Here is another example of an activity in which the demands of the processing involved may be sufficiently great to disrupt storage of crucial information in working memory. It is based on a working memory task known as reading span. The child is asked to read two short sentences, and after each one to say whether it is true or false. After the second sentence, the child attempts to recall the final words of each sentence, in order. Here are the sentences.

Dogs have four legs and bark.
Baby donkeys are called kittens.

The correct responses are: *true, false,* and *bark, kittens.* If the child responds correctly to two-sentence trials such as these, the number of sentences in the set will increase until the point (known as reading span) at which errors are made. The reading task alone will be challenging for many young children, and indeed for older children with reading difficulties. For example, they may struggle to identify the individual words in the sentences, or be slow in doing so, or indeed may have difficulty in accessing the knowledge that allows them to judge the veracity of the sentences. These processing difficulties will be demanding of working memory resources and, as a result, there will be little available to support memory for the final words.

The efficiency with which a child can carry out the processing is not the only determinant of working memory capacity, as memory performance between individuals often differs even if they have the same abilities to process material in a particular working memory task. The reason for this is that their working memory capacities are different.

The capacity to hold information in working memory is closely related to paying attention. Indeed, when you take part in a working memory activity, it feels as though you need to attend very hard to carry out the mental juggling needed to keep all of the information in mind. There are several different aspects to attention, which include the ability to focus on a particular activity for a sustained period of time, the ability to shut out (or 'inhibit') information that is irrelevant and potentially distracting, and also the ability to shift attention voluntarily between different activities. All of these kinds of attention are needed in working memory activities: it is necessary to keep focused on the particular information that is being remembered and processed, to inhibit information in order to minimise distractions that will lead to a neglect of the contents of working memory and so accelerated loss of information, and to switch rapidly between the processing and storage elements of a task in order to manage the mental juggling act.

Verbal short-term memory

Verbal short-term memory provides temporary storage for sound patterns of language. It can be used to store verbal items that are already familiar (words) and also items that have not previously been encountered, such as the word *coracle* that may be unfamiliar to a young child, or the word *graçias* being heard for the first time during a Spanish lesson in school. Verbal short-term memory consists of two different elements: a store and a rehearsal process. The information is held in a store whose contents decay very rapidly, usually in less than two seconds. This rapid decay can be prevented, at least for a short period of time, by rehearsing the material either aloud or silently. Rehearsal boosts the activation of the decaying contents, although because decay then sets in again rapidly it is necessary to rehearse continuously these contents in order to keep the information in short-term memory for longer periods. Whether rehearsal is effective or not is determined by how quickly the items you are trying to remember can be rehearsed. Because items in the store decay within about two seconds, it is necessary to rehearse all of them within this time to prevent them from decaying completely, and so being irretrievably lost. As we discussed in Chapter 1, because lengthy items such as *hippopotamus* or *dictionary* take longer to rehearse, they are more likely to be lost from verbal short-term memory than shorter words.

Although very young children can store verbal information, they do not typically rehearse until seven or eight years of age. As a result, young child lose information from verbal short-term memory very rapidly. When they do start to rehearse, the speed of rehearsal is relatively slow and this means that it is not as effective at recycling the contents of the store as in older children and adults.

Older children are also more effective at using long-term memory as a means of bolstering short-term memory performance. With increasing age and experience, the child's knowledge of the world (semantic memory) expands and incorporates increasingly complex connections between different words and concepts. As a consequence, the opportunities to boost working memory by grouping new information in meaningful ways that are related to knowledge in semantic memory are greatly increased. This use of long-term memory to support short-term memory performance and to alleviate working memory loads was discussed in more detail in Chapter 1, and is often known as chunking. For example, prior knowledge of the 'bird' category will make remembering this list of different birds much easier: *ostrich, parrot, sparrow, seagull*. Similarly, adults will find it much easier to remember the sequence *tuberculosis, palindrome, simultaneous* than four-year-old children simply because they are likely to be familiar with the meanings and labels of the words. This means that it will not be necessary to accurately store all of the sounds in each word, because they are already stored in our mental lexicon.

Visuo-spatial short-term memory

Visuo-spatial short-term memory is involved in recalling shape, orientation and other visual features of objects, as well as patterns of movements. An important change that takes place at about seven or eight years of age is that children develop a strong preference for using verbal short-term memory to remember visuo-spatial material where possible, such as expressing the information to be remembered in terms of its spoken name. Consider an activity in which the child views a set of three familiar objects (a comb, a toy pig and a fork) and then attempts to remember them when they have been removed from view. This is very similar to Kim's Game, a memory game that children like to play. Very young children, up to about seven years of age, will usually try to remember these objects by storing their images in visuo-spatial short-term memory. However, as they grow older they prefer to remember this information in terms of its verbal characteristics by rehearsing the names of the objects to be remembered (*comb, pig, fork*); this allows the sounds of these words to be held in verbal short-term memory. This is a more efficient way of remembering than relying purely on visuo-spatial short-term memory, and it leads to improvements in memory performance.

Measuring working memory

Measures of working memory – typically, forward and backward digit span – are included in most IQ-type standardised ability tests, and provide reasonable estimates of verbal short-term memory (forward digit span) and verbal working memory (backward digit span). However, usage of these test batteries is often restricted to individuals with psychometric training such as educational (school) psychologists and specialist teachers. These two measures also provide a relatively restricted assessment of working memory abilities, as they both use number-based material with which some children have particular difficulties. Furthermore, they provide no means of assessing short-term and working memory for visuo-spatial material. This is unfortunate because many children have weaknesses in some but not all components of working memory and their areas of strength can form the basis for effective use of compensatory strategies (see Chapter 5). Thus, a child with poor verbal working memory but good visuo-spatial working memory capacity may be particularly successful in using strategies and memory aids that play to this area of strength, such as diagrams and other visual cues that prevent working memory failure. Unless visuo-spatial working memory is measured, though, it is not possible to identify this area of possible strength.

In order to overcome the shortcomings of existing methods for assessing working memory, we have recently developed the Automated Working Memory Assessment (AWMA) as an easy and reliable way of measuring all significant elements of working memory. It is a computer-based program that has a user-friendly interface and provides a convenient way of identifying children with working memory problems that is suitable for use by teachers with no prior experience of test administration. Test presentation and scoring is automated and it is suitable for use with individuals aged 4 to 22 years. Test scores are calculated by the computer program, and the child's detailed working memory profile and predicted areas of learning difficulties are also generated by the program.

The AWMA consists of three tests each of verbal short-term memory, visuo-spatial short-term memory, verbal working memory and visuo-spatial working memory. Administration of the full test takes approximately 40 minutes. There is also the option to use the AWMA Short Form. This takes only 10 minutes to complete and is highly suitable for screening large groups of children such as entire classes for potential memory problems.

In general, children with poor working memory tend to perform poorly on all of the working memory tests, irrespective of whether they involve verbal or visuo-spatial material. This fits well with the account of working memory described in Chapter 1, according to which the central executive is involved in processing and manipulating any kind of material, and so should contribute to both verbal and visuo-spatial working memory tasks. A child who has a poor central executive would therefore be expected to have deficits in both types of working memory assessment. However, this is not true for all children with working memory problems. Some children have a much more uneven profile, with greater impairments in working memory performance for either verbal or visuo-spatial material. For example, children with language impairments and dyslexia tend to have greater deficits in verbal working memory than visuo-spatial working memory, and children with motor coordination difficulties typically perform more poorly on the visuo-spatial than the verbal working memory measures. This is probably because they have basic deficits in processing material of that particular kind which then has knock-on consequences for storing that material in working memory. For these children, the result will be poor working memory for some but not all kinds of information. However, there is substantial variation in the working memory profiles even for children with these particular diagnoses, and the AWMA provides a convenient way of establishing working memory strengths as well as weaknesses. The strengths are particularly important because, as we shall see in Chapter 5, they provide an excellent basis for developing effective strategies that can compensate for areas of working memory weakness.

Working memory and IQ

One question that we are often asked is whether working memory is any different from a child's intelligence, or IQ. The answer is that it is although some of the ways of measuring IQ are strongly influenced by working memory. An individual's IQ score is calculated from performance on a variety of different mental activities, some of which involve language (such as tests of vocabulary) and some of which do not (for example, constructing patterns from building bricks). IQ scores are expressed with reference to the range of performance found in children of that particular age, with an IQ score of 100 corresponding to average performance, a score of 85 to low performance found only in the bottom 16% of children of that age, and a score of 115 corresponding to high performance found only in the top 16% of children. IQ scores are moderately associated with children's learning achievements, particularly in academic subjects such as reading and maths.

A child's working memory consists of three key elements – verbal short-term memory, visuo-spatial short-term memory, and working memory. In contrast, IQ does not measure a single kind of ability or set of abilities, but instead taps a relatively wide range of different abilities and then adds them up: it was this feature of IQ that led to it being termed an 'intellectual ragbag' by one leading psychologist. The IQ measure is a summary of many different abilities, whereas working memory tests assess the capacity of components of one particular memory system that are very well understood.

Another important difference between working memory and IQ concerns the extent to which they are influenced by a child's prior experiences. Many IQ subtests draw on knowledge or skills that have to have been already acquired at the time of the test for the child to be able to perform successfully. Thus, a child who has not already learned the meaning or label of a particular word such as *derogatory* will not be able to produce a satisfactory definition of the word in a vocabulary test, no matter how hard he or she tries. Unsurprisingly, performance on these kinds of knowledge-based measures is influenced by many of the background factors in a child's life, such as the linguistic environment of their home, the quality of their interactions with family, and their nursery and pre-school education.

Working memory performance, in contrast, is not limited by any knowledge or skill that a child may or may not have. The information to be stored and manipulated in working memory tests is designed to be equally unfamiliar to all individuals, so no individual has an advantage in this respect. So in working memory tasks such as backward digit recall and the reading span task described earlier in the chapter, it is very unlikely that any child will ever have had to do anything similar before or after. However, because the tasks are very simple they can be easily understood even by young children, who typically will succeed in the early parts of the tests that involve low memory loads. Thus the child will start to fail as the task progresses because the memory load exceeds their working memory, and not because they have not learned something previously. Success or failure in these tasks is therefore limited not by previous experiences and opportunities, but on the particular memory resources that can be mustered at that particular point in time. For this reason, working memory assessments provide relatively pure measures of a child's ability to remember and to learn that are culture-fair; unlike many elements of IQ tests, they are not associated with the socioeconomic status of the child's family, or with the nature of pre-school care, or with the cultural or linguistic environment of the home.

Despite these differences, there are some direct correspondences between working memory and IQ assessments, and many children with poor working memory have low IQ and *vice versa*. In later chapters, we argue that working memory problems place serious limits on a child's abilities to learn, and as verbal IQ subtests in particular tap children's existing knowledge (for example, of vocabulary) working memory skills would also be expected to influence these components of IQ. Also, one influential test of intelligence, the Wechsler Intelligence Scales for Children, has now been modified to include several working memory subtests: scores on the new working memory subscale contribute strongly to the full-scale score calculated for the child. These newer kinds of IQ assessment are therefore both directly and indirectly influenced by working memory.

POINTS TO REMEMBER

- Working memory capacity increases from childhood through to adolescence, when adult levels are reached.

- Within a particular age group, there is wide variation in working memory capacity between individuals. In a classroom of seven-year-olds, some children will have the working memory capacities of the average five-year-old child, and others of an average eleven-year-old.

- Children typically start to use rehearsal in verbal short-term memory at about seven years of age, and at this age also shift towards preferring to remember information in terms of verbal characteristics if possible.

- Increases in working memory capacity with age relate to improvements in the efficiency of processing and of attention.

- The Automated Working Memory Assessment provides a convenient computer-based way of assessing children's working memory strengths and weaknesses which can be used to identify and guide effective learning support strategies.

- Working memory is related to but distinct from IQ, and because it is independent of factors relating to the child's background and learning opportunities it provides a relatively pure measure of learning ability.

CHAPTER 3

Working memory and learning

Overview

This chapter describes evidence that working memory capacity is closely related to children's abilities to learn. Working memory capacity is strongly associated with academic attainments in key areas of the curriculum such as reading and maths, from the earliest point at which children start school through to adolescence. Assessing working memory in young children also provides an effective way of identifying children at risk of poor educational achievements in later years. Ways in which working memory supports classroom learning are described, prior to a more detailed consideration in Chapters 5 and 6.

Introduction

One highly consistent finding from many research studies over the past 25 years is that measures of working memory capacity are excellent predictors of children's academic attainments. Children with high working memory scores typically show excellent reading skills at all ages and also do very well on tests of mathematical ability. Conversely, children with relatively poor working memory scores tend to perform below average levels on these attainment measures. The relationship between working memory and academic achievement extends across the lifespan and is present to as strong a degree in college students as in young children just starting school.

In the sections that follow, the most important links between working memory and learning are described. The first studies investigate working memory in children who achieve different levels of attainment in key areas of the academic curriculum. Next, we consider the extent to which working memory assessments administered at school entry before formal instruction has started can help identify children at risk of poor academic progress in the subsequent years. Research on children with learning difficulties that require additional educational support are presented in the next section, in which the patterns of working memory strengths and weaknesses associated with particular learning difficulties are described. In the final section, the reasons why children with low working memory capacity struggle to learn are discussed.

Working memory and curriculum learning

In the UK, full-time education is compulsory for all children from 5 to 16 years of age, during which period all state schools are required to teach to a national curriculum in core subject areas of English (which includes reading and writing), maths and science. At three ages (6/7, 10/11 and 13/14 years), all children attending state schools must complete national tests in each of these areas. On the basis of their performance both on these tests and also in teacher assessments conducted over a longer period of time, the children's attainments are expressed in terms of nationally expected levels.

Across a series of research studies, we have investigated the link between children's attainment levels on these national curriculum tests and their working memory abilities. In one research study, we assessed six- and seven-year-old children shortly after they had completed their national curriculum assessments on measures from the Working Memory Test Battery for Children. This is a comprehensive working memory assessment developed by Dr Susan Pickering, of the University of Bristol, England, with Susan Gathercole that includes tests of verbal short-term memory, visuo-spatial short-term memory, and verbal working memory. It is suitable for use with children aged from 4 to 15 years. Children's performances on the various tests in the battery are expressed as standard scores, in which a score of 100 corresponds to the average for that age group, with a standard deviation of 15. This means that the majority of children in an age group (68%) will receive a score that falls within between 86 and 115. Standard scores in the range of 70 to 85 are relatively poor for that age, with only 14% of the children in the population expected to score at this level. A standard score of less than 70 is extremely low, with only 2% of children scoring at this level. Above average performance is represented by standard scores in the range of 116 and 130, with a further 14% of the population falling within this range of performance. A standard score of more than 130 is extremely high, with only 2% of the population scoring at this level.

Figure 3.1 summarises the findings of this research study, showing the average verbal short-term memory and verbal working memory scores of the children grouped according to whether their performances on the national curriculum tests in English were below average, average or above average. The tests contributing to this classification were all literacy-based, involving reading, reading comprehension and spelling. The results are very clear. Working memory scores, shown as black bars in the figure, were lowest in the below average group, at average levels (approximately 100) for the average ability group, and high for the above average ability group. Short-term memory scores, shown as grey bars in the figure, did not differ between the three ability groups to the same degree, with the low ability group scoring at the same level as the average group. These findings, showing that working memory ability is a better predictor of academic abilities in areas such as reading than short-term memory ability, have been obtained in many research studies, and are important in establishing that it is working memory capacity in general, rather than short-term storage more specifically, that limits children's abilities to learn.

Consider now the memory scores of the same children re-grouped according to their attainment levels in maths rather than English. The results are summarised in Figure 3.2. These levels were based on a combination of tests that tap the children's abilities in number and algebra, and in the areas of shape, space and measurement. Once

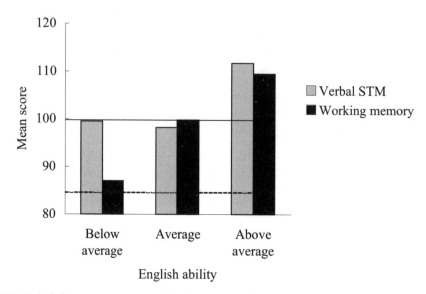

Figure 3.1 *Verbal short-term memory and working memory scores of six- and seven-year-old children grouped according to English attainment level. The solid line corresponds to average scores for this age and the dashed line to low scores of 85 and below.*

again, working memory scores were closely linked with the children's attainment levels. The low maths ability group obtained very low working memory scores, the average maths ability group had mid-range working memory scores that were entirely appropriate for their age, and the high ability group obtained above average working memory scores. As in the English ability groupings, verbal short-term memory scores did not differ between the low and average ability groups, although highest scores were obtained for the above average maths group.

The differences found in working memory between the ability groups in this study, in both English and maths, were large. In the low English ability groups, 41% of the children obtained working memory scores of 85 and below, a low level of achievement that we would only expect for 16% of children of this age. For the low maths ability group, the corresponding number obtaining standard scores at or below 85 was 52%. Poor working memory is much more common in children making poor academic progress than in the school population at large.

Research with older groups of children has established that the close

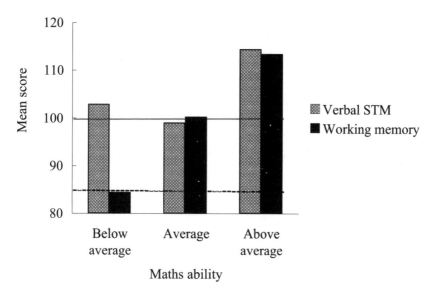

Figure 3.2 *Verbal short-term memory and working memory scores of six- and seven-year-old children grouped according to attainment levels in maths. The solid line corresponds to average scores for this age and the dashed line to low scores of 85 and below.*

association between working memory and academic progress extends far beyond these early years of education. In one study, we assessed the working memory abilities of children who had recently completed their final national curriculum assessments at 14 years of age. The English assessments at this age consisted of a reading and writing paper in which the children answered questions on two written passages, and a second paper required an essay answering a question about a scene from a Shakespeare play that had been studied by the children in class. These tests therefore evaluated the quality of the children's comprehension and interpretation of literary pieces of work, and of the complexity and maturity of the written language used by the children. The maths assessments consisted of two written tests of mathematical ability (one of which allowed the use of a calculator), and included some context-free short mathematical combinations employing the four basic arithmetic operations. In science, children are tested on their knowledge and understanding of the core topics studied in the previous three years of school.

The results of this study are shown in Figure 3.3, which shows the average working memory scores of the children grouped according to ability in each of the three subject areas. In each case, children with higher attainment levels had higher working memory scores. The biggest working memory differences by far were seen across the maths and science ability groups, with the children in the respective below average groups obtaining extremely low mean scores of around 77. Scores this low would only be expected in 6% of the general population. In contrast, the below average English group obtained a mean working memory score of 88; this corresponds to the lowest 22% in the population and represents low average rather than very poor memory abilities.

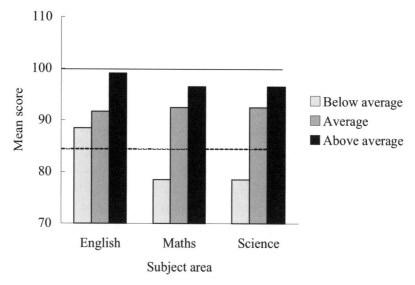

Figure 3.3 *Working memory scores of children grouped according to attainment levels in English, maths and science at 13 and 14 years. The solid line corresponds to average scores for this age and the dashed line to low scores of 85 and below.*

Working memory capacity therefore appears to limit the rate of learning in the late as well as early and middle years of compulsory education, particularly in maths and science. Other research with children completing their national curriculum assessments at 11 years has also established close links between working memory capacity and school attainments in English, maths and science. Later in this chapter, the specific contributions that working memory makes to learning in these academic areas are discussed.

Using working memory to identify children at risk of poor academic progress

Assessment of children's working memory abilities very early in their school career provides a highly effective way of identifying individuals who are at high risk of making poor academic progress in the following years. Early identification is important, as it allows the opportunity for prompt intervention that can minimise the adverse consequences of poor working memory capacity on learning (see Chapter 5).

We have recently demonstrated the value of routine screening of working memory at school entry to identify children at high risk of low educational achievements several years later, in a research study of approximately 500 children in schools in the North of England. Within six weeks of joining school at four years of age, the children completed assessments of working memory and verbal short-term memory. Approximately 30 months later, at six and seven years of age, they completed the national curriculum assessments of reading, writing and maths.

As in the research described in the previous section, we grouped the children as either below average, average, or above average according to their attainment levels in these later national curriculum tests. The difference is that in this study, the working memory scores that are calculated for each group were based on their assessments two and a half years previously, as they started school.

The results summarised in Figure 3.4 are remarkably similar to those found in our previous studies except that this time, the working memory measures were obtained several years earlier. In reading, writing and maths, children who failed to reach the national expected levels had obtained lower working memory scores at school entry at the age of four than those who reached average levels, who in turn obtained lower working memory scores than the children with attainment levels that exceeded the national average. The group differences were large in all areas but greatest of all for maths, with the below average group scoring about 20 points less than the above average group.

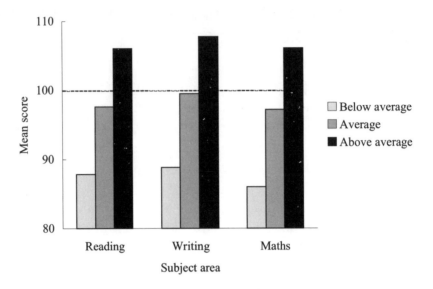

Figure 3.4 *Working memory scores at four years of children grouped according to attainment levels in English, maths and science 30 months later at six and seven years.*

In order to establish how well working memory scores at school entry could identify the individuals who would later fail to meet nationally expected levels of attainment, we grouped the children according to whether the working memory score at school entry was 86 and above (average) or 85 and below (low). The numbers of children in the low and average working memory groups with later attainments that were below the nationally expected levels were then calculated. In the low working memory group, 27% of the children performed below nationally expected levels in reading, 30% in writing and 8% in maths. The corresponding percentages of children obtaining working memory scores above 85 at school entry were 4% for reading, 4% for writing and 1% for maths. Thus, children with low working memory scores were seven times more likely than those with average working memory scores to fail to reach expected levels in each of reading, writing and maths.

So, working memory assessments taken at a very early point in time – at four or five years, using tests that take no longer than 15 minutes to complete – are extremely good predictors of what sort of academic progress the children will make over the coming two or three years of full-time education. Although about three-quarters of children with very low scores will achieve age-appropriate levels of learning in literacy and maths at this later point, there is a far higher proportion of these children who will not manage to reach these levels of achievement than in the remaining children with typical working memory capacities when they start school. Screening children at this early point before formal education begins in earnest therefore provides an excellent means of identifying those individuals at risk of poor learning achievement in the key academic areas of literacy and maths. On the basis of evidence reviewed earlier, that links between working memory and learning extend to at least 14 years of age, and also to progress in science, it seems likely that low working memory capacity at this early point represents a risk factor for low achievement across all years of formal education.

Working memory in children with learning difficulties

If children with poor working memory struggle to make good progress in key subject areas of the school curriculum, it might be expected that many of the children with learning difficulties in these areas will perform very poorly on measures of working memory. We have explored this possibility in research studies involving children recognised by their schools as having special educational needs (SEN). In the UK, there are formal processes for recognising and supporting children who have learning difficulties, with children classified according both to the nature and severity of their needs. More severe needs attract additional resources for the school from the local education authority, which are then used to support the learning needs of the child within school.

The opportunity to conduct our first study (Gathercole and Pickering) with children with SEN was provided by our development of the Working Memory Test Battery for Children. In order to standardise scores, all ten tests in the battery were administered to a large sample of children aged 4 to 15 years of age, drawn from a nationally representative set of schools. In addition to tests of working memory and verbal short-term memory, the battery also contained tests of visuo-spatial short-term memory, allowing assessment of all three components of the working memory model described in Chapter 1.

The schools participating in the study were asked to identify which children were recognised as having SEN and, if so, what their particular areas of educational difficulties were. Of the 750 children participating in the study, 98 (13%) had SEN. After the test scores had been standardised, we looked at the particular difficulties of these children and grouped them together if they had the same area of special need. For each of these subgroups of children with SEN, we then calculated their scores on each test in the battery. The main purpose of this study was to establish whether children who were making sufficiently poor progress in reading and maths to be recognised as SEN would score poorly on the working memory tests, and also to see how they performed on measures of verbal and visuo-spatial short-term memory. We also wanted to know whether working memory problems were characteristic of any other SEN subgroups in this sample.

Four main subgroups of children with SEN were identified from the sample. There was i) a small group of children whose problems were described as being related to language, and larger numbers of children with ii) difficulties that were specific to reading, iii) problems in both reading and maths, and iv) emotional and behavioural problems that were not cognitive in origin. For each subgroup, the mean working memory, verbal short-term memory and visuo-spatial short-term memory scores were calculated, and these are shown in Figure 3.5.

Different educational needs were associated with distinct profiles of working memory strength and weaknesses. The children with problems that extended across both reading and maths had the poorest working memory function, with low scores in each of the three aspects of working memory. This group therefore had no identifiable areas of strength across the different elements of working memory. The children with primary difficulties relating to language also had extremely poor working memory and verbal short-term memory scores, but their visuo-spatial memory scores were much higher, well within the average range. The third subgroup was composed of children who had reading problems without significant difficulties in

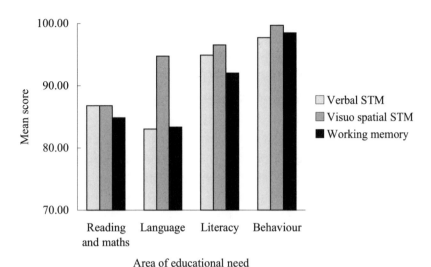

Figure 3.5 *Working memory scores of children with different areas of educational need.*

maths. These children performed in the low average range for all three aspects of working memory, and did not show the severe and pervasive working memory problems that characterised the children with both reading and maths problems. Finally, the children with emotional and behavioural problems performed at age-appropriate levels in all areas of working memory.

These findings have been influential in shaping our thinking about the ways in which working memory constrains children's learning. The most important result is that children who struggle in the two most significant areas of the school curriculum – reading and maths – have the poorest working memory profiles, with low scores in all three areas of working memory function. This fits well with results discussed in previous sections showing that individuals with low working memory make poor progress in both reading and maths. These children show no significant areas of working memory strength: they not only struggle in complex activities that combine storage with effortful processing (working memory tasks), but are also poor at storing either verbal or visuo-spatial material in short-term memory, providing few opportunities for compensatory strategies within working memory. The learning pathway through school for an individual with this profile is likely to be fraught with difficulty. It is important to note that the same pervasive working memory problems are not present in the majority of the children whose problems are specific to literacy and do not extend to maths. Rather, learning difficulties in both reading and maths appear to be a hallmark of poor working memory function. Chapter 4 describes in more detail the characteristics of these children and the problems that they face in the classroom.

The working memory profiles of the children with language learning problems are particularly interesting. These children have problems only in tests that involve verbal material: the working memory tests, which are all verbal in nature in the Working Memory Test Battery for Children, and the verbal short-term memory tests. Their problems on these tests are marked, greater in severity even than those of the 'classic' low working memory children discussed above. Their strengths in visuo-spatial memory do, however, provide a substantial basis to build compensatory strategies to facilitate classroom learning, as discussed in Chapter 5.

Because problems with reading and maths appear to be a developmental hallmark of poor working memory capacity, we identified a further sample of children identified by their schools as having reading difficulties. The main purpose of this study was to determine whether working memory was disproportionately impaired in these children, or was instead part of a more general cognitive deficit. Each child was therefore assessed on measures of IQ, language and phonological awareness, as well as working memory.

The results are summarised in Figure 3.6, which shows the proportion of this sample of children who had low or very low scores on each measure. The two measures on which the majority of children obtained low or very low scores were visuo-spatial short-term memory and working memory, with 70 – 80% of the children obtaining scores in this range. Low IQ scores were found for a substantial minority of the sample, but were less common than low working memory scores. Poor performance on the tests of language, verbal short-term memory and phonological awareness were found in even fewer of the children. Thus the working memory deficits of this sample of children with reading difficulties could not be explained simply in terms of more general cognitive impairments of either IQ or language abilities.

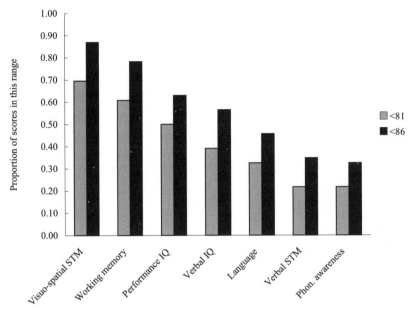

Figure 3.6 *Proportions of children with reading difficulties obtaining low (<86) and very low (<81) standard scores on measures of cognitive ability*

Further evidence that the severity of learning difficulties is strongly influenced by the extent to which working memory capacity is impaired was provided in a study of children aged 7 to 11 years who were identified by their schools as having learning difficulties in the absence of sensory, physical or behavioural difficulties. Each child was at one of the three stages of assessment and provision of special educational support, as specified by the UK Code of Practice (DfEE). At the first stage, School Action, a teacher or special needs coordinator identifies a child who needs additional or different support from that provided within the general curriculum. At the next assessment stage, School Action Plus, the school requests assistance from an external specialist to meet the child's needs. In the final stage, children who require additional resources to support their learning needs will be issued a statement of special educational needs. The stage at which each child had reached on the Code of Practice therefore provides an index of the severity of their learning difficulties although, as children may proceed through successive stages across time, it is an approximate measure.

Although working memory scores were found to be low for all of these children, scores declined with more advanced stages of the Code of Practice: the average score was 80 for a child on School Action, 77 for a child on School Action Plus, and 70 for a child with a statement of special educational needs. A score of 70 is extremely low and is found in less than 3% of the general population. The extent of a child's working memory problems therefore corresponded closely to the severity of their learning difficulties in reading and maths.

The research in this chapter establishes that children with learning difficulties in reading and in maths typically have very poor working memory capacities. The key question that follows from the research reviewed in this chapter is: why is working memory so closely related to learning? In the next section, we try to answer this question.

Working memory overload impairs learning

The learning difficulties faced by children with poor working memory arise because they are unable to meet the working memory demands of many potential learning situations. As a consequence, their working memory becomes overloaded and the crucial information that is needed to guide the ongoing activity – such as the sentence they are attempting to write, or the sequence of instructions they need to follow – is lost. Chapter 1 described this process of the loss of information from working memory as catastrophic, because it cannot subsequently be recovered. In this situation, it will not be possible for the child to proceed with the activity and to see it through to a successful conclusion unless he or she is able to access again the critical task information that is needed. The child is therefore forced either to guess at this point (a strategy that is likely to lead to errors) or to abandon the task before its completion.

Learning activities in the classroom are designed to support the child in the gradual accumulation of knowledge and skill defined by the curriculum so that over many years they become competent in domains such as reading and maths. Activity failures that are caused by loss of information that is crucial to the ongoing task from working memory represent missed learning opportunities for the child. The more frequent these failures are, the more that learning will be delayed. In this respect, poor working memory capacity provides a relatively general constraint on progress that would be expected to affect the rate of learning in any curriculum area that imposes substantial demands on mental storage and processing, such as science as well as literacy and maths. In more practical subjects such as art and music, poor working memory is less likely to hinder a child's progress.

We have obtained direct evidence that structured learning activities often place excessive demands on working memory for many individuals from our observations of low working memory children in their regular classroom setting. Many regular classroom activities require the child to hold in mind substantial amounts of information, often while completing another mental activity that also demands attention. Low memory children frequently made errors on these tasks and failed to complete them. Often, we saw direct evidence that they had forgotten crucial information – they would even ask a child sitting next to them, or even on occasion the observer, to repeat something to them. Some kinds of situations were particularly problematic for the children with poor working memory. They struggled to follow lengthy and complex instructions, often completing the first step or possibly the first two correctly, and then giving up. They also had great difficulties when the activity involved processing some information and remembering other material at the same time. The children also often lost their places in complex tasks. Sentence writing in younger children often led to place-keeping difficulties: typically, children would concentrate on spelling a word and then forget their location in the sentence, resulting in either skipping or repeating words if, that is, they could still remember the sentence, which they often could not.

More detailed illustrations of these and other features of the classroom behaviour of children with poor working memory are provided in Chapters 4 and 5. The important point here is that these many classroom situations in which low working memory children fail will inevitably slow the rates at which they can accumulate the bedrock of knowledge and skills in key academic domains. It is crucial that such children are supported to help them overcome this obstacle, and Chapters 5 and 6 focus on ways that this can be achieved.

POINTS TO REMEMBER

- Children's progress in reading, maths and science is closely related to their working memory capacities, across the full range of school years.

- Measures of working memory as children start formal education are effective predictors of reading and maths abilities several years later, and can be used to identify individuals who are at risk of poor educational progress in the subsequent school years.

- Children with learning difficulties in reading and maths typically have very poor working memory capacities, and their memory scores predict the severity of their learning problems.

- Poor working memory performance does not appear to be due to more general factors such as low IQ or language difficulties.

- The poor rates of learning in children with low working memory capacities are due in large part to memory overload in structured learning activities, which causes them to forget crucial information and so to fail in these tasks.

CHAPTER 4

Children with poor working memory

Overview

In this chapter, the main characteristics of children with poor working memory are outlined: their general behaviour, poor academic progress and the difficulties they face in classroom learning activities. These difficulties include failing to follow instructions, problems with activities that combine storage and processing, place-keeping difficulties and attentional problems. Particular areas of difficulty are illustrated with examples taken from our classroom observations.

Introduction

Nathan is in his second year of full-time education. He is a quiet child who is well-behaved in the classroom and is relatively popular with his peers. He has been placed in the lowest ability groups in both reading and maths. His teacher feels that he often fails to listen to what she says to him, and says that she often feels that he is 'in a world of his own'.

In class, Nathan struggles to keep up with many classroom activities. For example, when the teacher wrote on the board 'Monday 11th November' and, underneath, 'The Market', which was the title of the piece of work, he lost his place in the laborious attempt to copy the words down letter by letter, writing *moNemarket*. It seemed that he had begun to write the date, forgot what he was doing and began writing the title instead. He also frequently failed to complete structured learning activities. In one instance, when the teacher handed Nathan his computer login cards and told him to go and work on the computer numbered 13, he failed to do this because he had forgotten the number. On another occasion, Nathan was encouraged to use a number line when counting the number of ducks shown on two cards but struggled to coordinate the act of jumping along the line with counting up to the second number. He abandoned the attempt, solving the sum instead by counting up the total number of ducks on the two cards.

Nathan struggles with tasks that combine mental processing demands with the storage of several items at once. For example, when asked to identify two rhyming words in a four-line text read aloud by the teacher, he was unable to match the sound structures of the pair of words, store them and then recall them when the teacher finished reading the text.

Nathan is six years old and has poor working memory. He has not been diagnosed as having a developmental disorder of any kind, and at this point in his second year of full-time schooling has not been identified as having any special educational needs. In the years to come, however, he may well be considered to have specific learning difficulties. Despite this apparently unremarkable profile, children like Nathan are at high risk of poor educational achievement over the next decade of education, and of entering adult life with few academic qualifications. Early recognition of these problems and the provision of appropriate educational support over the coming years are vital to their future achievements.

Nathan is one of many children who have taken part in our research studies and his profile is typical. He came to our attention because he scored very poorly on working memory a few weeks after starting school at five years. His performance IQ (a measure of general cognitive ability based on measures that do not involve language) was in the average range. Just over a year later, a member of our research team spent a week observing Nathan in the course of his regular classroom activities. By this point, we knew that children with low working memory scores struggled markedly with academic learning, but wanted to find out why. To do this, it was necessary to find out exactly what was going wrong for these children at the point of learning: when they were in the classroom.

The purpose of this chapter is to describe what we have learned about the characteristics of children with poor working memory. By recognising these characteristics, it is possible even without formal assessments to identify the children who are likely to have learning difficulties related to working memory. Understanding the particular problems the children face and why their learning progress is so poor is a necessary step towards effectively supporting them and improving their learning outcomes. Ways of helping these children are discussed and illustrated in Chapter 5.

General characteristics

More boys than girls have poor working memory. In our studies, the ratio of boys to girls with working memory scores that fall in the lowest 10% for their age is 3:2, although in the population as a whole boys and girls do not differ on working memory tests. Both boys and girls typically show little variability in the severity of their problems from day to day. They consistently perform at low levels on measures of working memory, and also experience the same classroom-based problems on a daily basis.

Although children with poor working memory usually have normal social relationships with their peers, they are often relatively reserved in larger group activities within the classroom, particularly in teacher-led discussions such as 'carpet-time' that involve the whole class of children. Often, these discussions are based around a book that the teacher has read to the class, or other activities in which the children have recently been engaged. In these situations, the children rarely volunteer information when the teacher asks questions of the group as a whole. On some occasions, a child raises his or her hand to answer the question, but is unable to answer it when asked to do so by the teacher. Whether the child originally has an answer in mind and has forgotten it is unclear. Often, low memory children do not fully engage with the ongoing group discussions, and become withdrawn or distracted. The typical classroom behaviour of two boys is described below.

Luke (aged 9) is extremely reserved in both whole-class and group activities. He reluctantly answers direct questions, tending to use gestures such as shrugging his shoulders or nodding his head to denote a response. When Luke does respond verbally, it is usually in response to fairly simple tasks. Likewise, he rarely volunteers information or answers. On occasions when he does raise his hand to make a response, he often doesn't know what to say. For instance, Luke volunteered to explain how to recognise odd numbers in a numeracy lesson but was unable to do so when finally asked.

Declan (6 years) is a reserved and quiet child who tends not to volunteer responses and rarely answers direct questions, particularly in the whole-class situation. He sometimes becomes more vocal when working in small groups although he isn't necessarily discussing the task in hand.

What do teachers say about the children? They describe them as making poor academic progress, having short attention spans and high levels of distractibility, as failing to monitor adequately the quality of their work, and showing a lack of creativity in solving complex problems. They also judge the majority of the children to have either very low or vulnerable levels of self-esteem. Teachers also believe that the children feel unable to exercise control over their environment, which can cause frustration and low levels of motivation. Some of these features are described in more detail in the following sections.

Poor academic progress

Parents and teachers often ask how likely it is that a child who has been identified as having poor working memory will struggle with academic learning in school. Unfortunately, the answer is that it is very likely. We have recently completed a large-scale screening study of over several thousand children in which we identified individuals who scored very poorly on two working memory tests from the Automated Working Memory Assessment (AWMA). The tests were administered by computer and took about ten minutes to complete (Chapter 2 provides more information on assessing working memory and the AWMA).

Approximately 300 children aged five/six and nine/ten years with poor working memory (in the bottom 10% for their age group) were identified in this way. In both age groups, the majority of children were struggling academically. In the younger group, 75% of the children scored at very low levels in both reading and maths, and a further 5% obtained low scores only in maths. In the older group, 68% of the children obtained very low scores in reading and 71% in maths; together, 83% of the children showed poor progress in either reading or maths.

Poor working memory therefore places a child at a high risk of slow rates of academic progress, with four out of five children achieving unusually low scores in measures of literacy and numeracy, the foundations of the school curriculum. Even within a year of starting school, the majority of the children will have been identified by their teachers as struggling in reading and maths, and will be working in the lowest ability groups in these areas.

Chapter 3 described how the slow academic progress of these children arises in large part because they are unable to cope with the working memory demands of many of the classroom activities that are designed to help them learn. This leads to frequent failures in many of the episodes that should provide them with new opportunities to learn, and results in a slow and uneven pace of curriculum learning which is greatest in subject areas such as reading and maths that impose high loads on working memory. Later in this chapter and in Chapter 5 we provide illustrations of what can happen when working memory is overloaded in this way.

Working memory can limit learning in these areas in a number of ways. Consider first learning to read. Children must learn the spelling patterns of individual words (a process known as establishing a sight vocabulary). They must also master the rules of phonics (the mappings between sounds in the language and both individual letters and letter combinations) in order to be able to recognise and spell words that have not yet entered their sight vocabulary. Children with poor working memory are slow to learn the mappings between the sounds of familiar words and their print patterns, and this impairs their abilities to read and to spell individual words. This learning difficulty arises because the children often fail in the classroom activities designed to build up basic literacy knowledge, due to their inability to meet the heavy working memory loads of many of these activities. These frequent failures will inevitably slow down the incremental process of learning to read.

To be literate, the child also needs to extract meaning – represented by the relationships between the printed words – from text. In fact in most situations, the goal of reading is comprehension. Working memory plays an important role in this process too, by holding the words that have been recognised from print for a sufficient period of time to enable the reader to link the words together to produce a meaningful interpretation of the clause or sentence, or even of larger sections of text. Children with low working memory capacity struggle to meet the storage demands of this process of interpretation as well as to recognise the individual printed words. As a result, they have even greater problems in understanding text than in simply reading individual words or in spelling, because this additional process of interpretation is also limited by working memory.

In maths, these children typically have particular difficulties in performing the basic arithmetic number operations of addition, subtraction, division and multiplication. There are several reasons for this. First, working memory overload in the individual activities designed to develop numeracy skills will result in frequent errors and task failures, impairing the incremental process of acquiring basic number skills and knowledge, and slowing down the child's rate of learning. Second, mental arithmetic is heavily dependent on working memory, as discussed in Chapter 1: it requires not only the storage of arbitrary numerical information, but also the retrieval and application of number rules that may not yet have been securely learned. These conditions of combined storage and mental processing are the hallmark of activities that place heavy demands on working memory, and the child with a low working memory capacity will encounter great difficulties in meeting these demands. The errors in mental calculations that will result from the loss of information in working memory will inevitably provide very poor conditions for the child to acquire number knowledge and rules. Poor progress in learning basic number facts will exacerbate these problems, as children are forced to rely on rudimentary strategies that require a high degree of attention, such as finger-counting, rather than being able to retrieve knowledge that has already been learned and highly practised (see Chapter 5). The use of such strategies in itself generates an increased burden on working memory in individuals with working memory capacity.

The majority of children with low working memory are considered by their teachers to be poor at monitoring the quality of their work. They are often described as failing to check work for mistakes, making careless errors, producing work that is sloppy and being poor in organising their written work. There may be two reasons for this. One is the academic ability in a particular academic domain, which will probably be fairly low. The work produced by a child who is struggling to learn to read and write is likely to appear shoddy because of the difficulty with which it is produced, and the high number of errors it probably contains. The second likely cause of monitoring problems is the forgetting of crucial information that is needed to guide a task through to completion. Thus, the child may forget the sentence that he or she is attempting to write (for example, *Guy Fawkes attempted to blow up the Houses of Parliament with gunpowder*), or the particular patterns of numbers in a sequence that he or she is trying to generate (for example, *starting with 3, add on three to each number until you have filled all of the boxes on the sheet*). In these circumstances, the child may not be able to see the task through to completion even with errors, due to high levels of forgetting. As a final check of whether the work is correct or not requires the child to compare what has been done with the original instruction, it is probably out of the question. As we shall see in the next section, remembering and following instructions represents one of the major challenges faced by children with poor working memory.

Classroom difficulties

This section describes the specific kinds of classroom situations which cause difficulties and task failures in children with poor working memory, and that contribute to their low rates of academic learning.

Failure to follow instructions

Instructions are the basic currency of the classroom: throughout the school day, the teacher needs to communicate as efficiently as possible with the pupils what has to be done, by whom, in what way and in what order. Sometimes, the instruction involves the physical management of the children and their work objects in the classroom, as in the following example drawn from our classroom observations.

> 'Stop what you are doing. Put your hands on your knees. Now tidy your tables. Stand up behind your chair when you've finished. Put your hands by your side.'

Other instructions relate to a sequence of actions in a learning activity, as in this example.

> 'First of all, take the green cube. Next, put the red cube on the tower. The third cube should be orange. The fourth one is blue. The last one is brown. Let me see your tower. Is it like mine?'

Some instructions supply crucial information that is intrinsic to a particular activity, and that involves the preservation of a high level of detail that is needed for accurate performance. Here is an example.

> 'Count the pictures with me to find out how many pies there are (three). Imagine you eat one of the pies so cross one off. How many pies are left?(2) Now help me to write that as a sum.'

These commands impose working memory loads that are quite significant even for an older child or adult, so it is perhaps not too surprising that one of the most consistent and substantial types of problems faced by children with poor working memory is in following instructions. Here are some examples of failures of children with poor working memory to follow general classroom management instructions.

> Rhys (eight years) was sent as the first pupil to line up at the door in preparation for the lunch break but instead of waiting by the door he

began to walk straight out of the classroom.

The teacher asked the class to 'Put your sheets on the green table, arrow cards in the packet, put your pencil away and come and sit on the carpet.' John (six years) moved his sheets as requested, but failed to do anything else. When he realised that the rest of the class was seated on the carpet, he went and joined them, leaving his arrow cards and pencil on the table.

Sita (six years) was participating in a word activity in the literacy hour in which the teacher was showing flashcards to the children to remind them of the high frequency words they had previously learnt. The children were asked to stop the teacher as he shuffled through the cards when he had reached a specific word. Sita, however, stopped the teacher on every card he showed rather than on the specified word.

The following examples show that children also often forget the detailed content that is crucial to ongoing classroom activities. In these cases, forgetting leads to task failure for the child, and represents another missed opportunity for learning. Consider the following notes from our observations.

In a task involving the use of colour to identify the first/third/last flower in a line of ten pictures, Liam (six years) coloured the flowers at random rather than following the teacher's instructions: 'Take a coloured pencil, colour the first flower on the sheet, take another pencil, point to the third flower. Now colour it.'

Keisha (ten years) sometimes needed prompting to remind her of instructions previously given. On one occasion, she was praised for beginning to list the acronyms down the left-hand side of the page but had to be reminded to go back and match the correct meanings to the words. She also failed to remember to provide information about an extra acronym that was written on the worksheet (TV), for which the meaning had not been provided.

At the beginning of a literacy lesson when the children were focusing on work on letter blends, the teacher reviewed work that the children had completed on the *sn* blend and asked them to provide examples of words beginning with this blend. John confidently suggested the word *snake*. The teacher then introduced the new blend, *sp*, giving examples of words beginning with the sound and modelling how to put them into a sentence, for example, *The speeding spider spied a spade*. Some of the pupils, including John, volunteered to suggest appropriate sentences. However, when John was asked to share his idea, he responded saying, *Bob*: he had forgotten the blend.

These are situations in which the child was unable to proceed properly with the ongoing classroom activity because crucial information about the task had been lost from working memory. In the first example, a consequence of forgetting is that Liam did not gain the benefits of developing and practising his knowledge of ordinal position (first/third/last) from this activity. In Keisha's case, the delay in matching up the words with their definitions prevented her from completing the whole list in the allotted time, and so deprived her of the full opportunities for developing her vocabulary knowledge that were gained by her peers. John did not gain practice in searching for words that contained the target blend, so missing an opportunity to develop further his phonological awareness. The working memory failures observed had consequences for many different kinds of learning, ranging from the child's developing facility with language through to knowledge and skills at handling print and numbers.

In a recent research study, we investigated in more detail the difficulties of children with poor working memory in following lengthy instructions. In this task, the children were given instructions such as *Touch the red pencil, then pick up the blue ruler and put it in the black box*, and then either instructed to perform the action sequence (by showing them a picture of a hand) or to repeat it (with a picture of a mouth). The results established that the problems of the low memory children were even more severe than we had anticipated. As expected, the low memory group was much poorer at carrying out the lengthier instruction than the group with average working memory. They were also many times more likely not to follow correctly the instruction either to perform or to repeat the instruction: typically, they would carry out the action even if the instruction had been to repeat it. Thus these children forgot what general action to perform as well as the detailed content of the instruction.

To help these children fare better in class, instructions can be broken down and made shorter so that all children can each complete one step at a time. They can also be made less complex by using language that is simple both in vocabulary and in phrasing. Judicious repetition delivered at the right point will benefit many children with poor working memory. Use of memory aids to represent the sequence of activities in a task will help, and so too may the employment of other devices such as audio recording devices and digital note pads to help the child retain essential information needed to guide them through an activity. Practical ways of reducing working memory loads, illustrated by case studies, are described in Chapter 5.

Problems with activities that combine storage and processing

The children also frequently fail to meet the memory demands of the many learning activities in which they have to keep something in mind while doing something else that is mentally challenging and demands their attention. The mental juggling involved in combining storage with effortful mental activity is highly demanding of working memory, as discussed in Chapter 1.

At the beginning of this chapter it was described how Nathan struggled in one such activity. The task was to identify the rhyming words in a text read aloud by the teacher, and the children had to wait until all four lines had been read before telling the teacher the two words that rhymed: *tie* and *fly*. This imposes a very heavy working memory load. The child must mentally register the words in each line of the poem as it is spoken, and store the lines while making mental comparisons of the sound structures of pairs of words from different lines. Nathan was unable to do this, although on a separate assessment of verbal short-term memory he was capable of remembering two words in order without error. It was the combined demands of the mental processing required to compare the rhyme patterns of pairs of words and the need to store the four lines of the poem, that made the working memory load of this task excessive for this child.

Here is a number-based activity that involves both storage and effortful mental process on which we have observed a child with low working memory to struggle. Ahmet's teacher wrote sequences of numbers on the white board such as 0, 1, 2, 4, 5, 7, 8 that had some numbers missing. She read aloud the numbers, and asked the class what numbers had been missed out. In each case, there was more than one number missing. In this task, the child must retrieve his or her number knowledge of number sequences to identify each missing number, and to store each number while continuing to check for missing numbers to the end of the sequence. This task therefore combines effortful mental processing (to identify the missing numbers) with storage (of the missing numbers identified so far). In each case, Ahmet was unable to name the missing numbers.

Another example of a classroom activity requiring both storage and mental processing that we observed involved counting the words in sentences. Olivia's group were given a sentence (*In the summer it is sunny*) and asked to count the words (six), and then to write the sentence, and finally to check that the number of words they had written was the same as the number of words that they had counted in the sentence. Olivia managed to count the words, but by the time she came to start writing the sentence she had forgotten it, and quickly abandoned the attempt. In this situation, counting the words demanded Olivia's full attention, distracting her from maintaining the sentence in working memory.

Chapter 5 describes practical ways of reducing the working memory loads of these kinds of activities, and of supporting children using memory aids and other strategies that reduce reliance on working memory.

Place-keeping difficulties

Children with poor working memory often have problems in keeping track of their progress in a particular activity. For children in the early stages of acquiring skills in academic domains such as literacy and numeracy in particular, navigating their way through tasks that seem very simple to an adult can be extremely demanding on working memory. Consider Nathan's attempt to write the date (*Monday 11th November*) and title (*The Market*) of a piece of work, described at the beginning of this chapter. His attempt to do this, writing *moNemarket*, reflected a series of errors in keeping track of his progress: he wrote the first two letters of the day of the week, followed by the capital letter of the month, and then shifted to copying the title.

Another example of place-keeping difficulties was provided by observation of Niall (five years) in a numeracy lesson. The children in Niall's group were engaged in a counting activity designed to promote skills in using a number line. They were shown two displays each containing a different number of cartoon ducks, and were asked to add up the number of ducks across the two displays. To do this, the child must count the number of ducks in the first display, locate the corresponding number on the number line, count the ducks in the second display, and then add this number on to the first total by moving the appropriate number of steps along the number line. Although Niall successfully counted the objects in the first display and found the corresponding starting point on the number line, he then erroneously re-counted the number of objects in the first display rather than the second and added this total on.

The repetition and skipping errors made by Nathan and Niall arise from their failures to remember how far they have progressed in a task, a problem that is clearly exacerbated by the mentally challenging activities in which the child has to engage in each case – writing individual words in Nathan's case, and counting in Niall's case. These place-keeping problems clearly share many features of the problems in following instructions and in coping with activities that combine storage with demanding mental processing that were described in the two previous sections. In each of these cases, a child with poor working memory is placed in a situation in which something has to be done – either mentally and/or physically – and the child must also temporarily store information (such as how far he or she had progressed in the task) to guide progress towards task completion. These conditions combine to yield a working memory load that for many children will be excessive and will inevitably lead to task failure.

Because losing track of progress in a complex activity almost inevitably leads to task failure – we have rarely observed cases of successful self-correction – it is important for classroom staff to identify ways of preventing place-keeping errors. With complex hierarchical task structures in which the child needs to repeatedly switch between different levels of activity, it can be very useful both to simplify the task and to provide the child with an opportunity to record his or her progress within the task. For example in Niall's case, in which the task involved two alternations between object counting and using the number line, he may have benefited from counting the objects in the two displays first and writing down the total, and then applying the two numbers to the number line (the first number representing the starting point, and the second one being the number of steps to count on). Other methods for supporting the problems encountered by children with poor working memory in keeping track of their place in complex task structures are described, accompanied by examples, in Chapter 5.

Attentional problems

When we ask teachers to describe pupils that we have identified through our routine screening programme as having poor working memory, they rarely say that they have memory problems. Instead, the majority of children are described as having short attention spans, as being easily distracted, as only paying attention to things he or she is really interested in, and having difficulties in concentrating. The following statements are typical: 'he's in a world of his own', 'he doesn't listen to a word I say', 'she's always day-dreaming', and 'with him, it's in one ear and out of the other'.

Our own observations also identified high levels of inattention and distractibility, as the following two examples show.

Declan (aged six) struggles to maintain attention, particularly during whole-class teaching when the pupils join together on the carpet. He sits directly in front of the teacher and is frequently prompted to sit correctly and to pay attention as he regularly fidgets, looks around the classroom and distracts other children near him. He requires constant individual attention to support him in his work and to ensure he remains on task as he easily loses his place in learning activities and often abandons tasks. For example,

Declan was the only pupil who hadn't calculated a simple addition during the mental maths session so his teacher worked directly with him, repeating the addition process for him. He also needed to be reminded to participate when the children were counting together as the teacher pointed to ascending numbers on the 100 square.

In class, Curtis (six years) tries hard to fully participate in learning activities but he often becomes frustrated with tasks and appears to lose interest and concentration, occasionally leading him to abandon tasks. For example, during group work in the literacy lesson, Curtis worked with four other children of similar ability to rehearse a short dramatic performance of *The Three Little Pigs*. The teacher guided the children as they volunteered to perform specific roles and discussed what their characters would be like. Curtis confidently took on an acting role and participated fairly well in the first part of the group discussion as he successfully remembered the key events in the story. However, he soon began to lose interest in the play rehearsal and stood with his hands in his pockets as the other pupils offered more detailed ideas for the performance.

The children struggle in particular to maintain their focus in ongoing activities that are mentally challenging. This profile fits very well with recent research on young adults by Professor Michael Kane at the University of North Carolina, USA. These individuals were supplied with electronic devices that bleeped at random at several points during each day, at which point they were required to rate their current behaviour on various dimensions. Individuals with low working memory spans were much more likely to engage in mind-wandering when engaged in demanding cognitive activities than individuals with more typical memory spans. This phenomenon, which Kane has termed 'zoning out', appears to be a hallmark of situations in which working memory is overloaded so that the individual is no longer able to keep in mind the information needed to guide an ongoing mental activity. It seems inevitable that these situations will occur more frequently in individuals with reduced working memory capacity.

Although the children typically do not have the highly elevated levels of hyperactive/impulsive behaviour that are characteristic of ADHD (Attention Disorder Hyperactivity Deficit), mild degrees of restlessness do sometimes accompany inattentive behaviour in children with poor working memory. This is illustrated by the following example.

> As the main part of the lesson developed, Dionne (ten years) became increasingly more distracted and appeared to lose total concentration. She began to swing on her chair, talk to her neighbour and shout out unrelated comments.

When the children start an activity, they typically do so in a purposeful manner, performing well in the early stages of a complex or lengthy activity, losing focus only after beginning to make errors. For this reason, it seems likely that inattentive and distractible behaviour is a consequence of working memory overload rather than a more basic failure to pay attention in the first place. Minimising working memory failures should lead to substantial improvements in the child's ability to maintain focused attention across the full course of a classroom activity.

This chapter has described the many ways in which a child's progress in learning activities can become error-prone and stall when working memory fails. These observations are the starting point for identifying ways of providing effective educational support, discussed in Chapters 5 and 6, that will prevent and overcome these causes of slow learning progress.

POINTS TO REMEMBER

Children with poor working memory typically have the following characteristics.

- Despite good social integration with their peers, they are often reserved in group situations.
- Their academic progress in reading and maths is slow.
- Their limited working memory capacities are frequently overloaded in structured learning activities, leading to failures to follow instructions, difficulties in completing tasks that combine storage and demanding mental processing, and problems in keeping track of their progress in complex tasks. These frequent task failures impair learning in key academic domains.
- The children appear to be inattentive and highly distractible, probably due to working memory overload and forgetting.

Classroom support for children with poor working memory

Overview

This chapter describes a classroom-based approach designed to min-imise working memory failures and enhance learning opportunities in children with working memory problems. The principles of the approach are grounded in cognitive theory and research and are outlined and illustrated with examples of classroom practice.

Introduction

Chapters 3 and 4 described the substantial learning difficulties faced by the majority of children with working memory problems. Here, we consider what steps can be taken to address the problems faced by these children and outline a classroom-based approach that we have developed with Professor Julian Elliott of the School of Education at the University of Durham, with the aim of learning in children with these problems.

The approach that we recommend for children with poor working memory can be stated simply: avoid working memory failures in order to prevent the child's learning from being delayed and impaired. To achieve this, it is often necessary to modify the structure of learning activities. With suitable changes, the child will be able to complete with success the classroom activities in which he or she previously struggled, and so can proceed with learning. A substantial strength of the approach is that it can be readily implemented within the context of the existing curriculum and methods of teaching. In the sections below, the basic principles of the working memory intervention are described, illustrated by examples from an ongoing research study employing the approach.

The intervention is guided by research and theory in cognitive psychology, and consists of seven core principles that aim to prevent task failures due to working memory overload. Experienced teachers will note that many of the approaches and strategies that are recommended reflect current good practice. In our observations of both regular classes and classes implementing the working memory intervention, we have seen many teaching staff adopt these strategies to good effect. Some of the excellent practice we have seen that targets working memory failures either directly or indirectly has now been incorporated into the intervention approach outlined here. This touchstone with current practice encourages us to believe that the principles and strategies are both useful and practicable in the classroom context.

What is novel about the working memory intervention is that a coordinated set of approaches and strategies sharing the common purpose of avoiding working memory load are focused directly on the child. This allows learning to take place within a rich network of support that compensates for poor working memory capacity, enabling the frequency of task failures to diminish, the child's confidence to improve, and the rate of learning to be enhanced. It is recommended that the principles are used both to guide the development of lesson plans and to monitor the child's performance in class, with the aim of minimising the likelihood that the child fails to complete the intended learning activity successfully due to working memory failures. The seven principles are described below, illustrated by examples of how they have been successfully implemented from our observations of the intervention project. The key features of the approach are summarised in Table 5.1.

Table 5.1 Principles of the working memory intervention

Principles	Further information
Recognise working memory failures	Warning signs include incomplete recall, failure to follow instructions, place-keeping errors and task abandonment
Monitor the child	Look out for warning signs and ask the child
Evaluate working memory loads	Heavy loads caused by lengthy sequences, unfamiliar and meaningless content, and demanding mental processing activities
Reduce working memory loads when necessary	Reduce the amount of material to be remembered, increase the meaningfulness and familiarity of the material, simplify mental processing and restructure complex tasks
Repeat important information	Repetition can be supplied by teachers or fellow pupils nominated as memory guides
Encourage use of memory aids	These incude wall charts and posters, useful spellings, personalised dictionaries, cubes, counters, abaci, Unifix blocks, number lines, multiplication grids, calculators, memory cards, audio recorders and computer software
Develop the child's own strategies to support memory	These include asking for help, rehearsal, note-taking, use of long-term memory, and place-keeping and organisational strategies

Principles of the working memory intervention

1 Recognise working memory failures

There are four main warning signs of working memory failure, and the individuals responsible for supporting the child's learning at a particular point in time (these may include teachers, learning support assistants, special needs coordinators, parent helpers and parents) must be able to detect the warning signs of working memory overload. If any signs are detected, the working memory demands of the task should be evaluated (see 3) in order to determine whether working memory overload is likely to be the cause. If the working memory demands of the task are significant, it is recommended that the activity should be repeated with a reduced working memory load. This can be achieved by the methods described in 4, 6, 7 and 8. The warning signs are as follows.

i) Incomplete recall
The child forgets some or all of the information that is required to complete successfully a particular task or activity. A typical example of this kind of error is that the child cannot remember the words in a sentence he or she is attempting to write. If forgetting is partial rather than complete, it is usually the case that the child remembers the information at the beginning – for example, the first few words in the sentence – but forgets the rest.

ii) Failure to follow instructions
One common type of working memory failure is that the child cannot remember and so does not follow multi-step instructions. The child may remember only part of the instruction (typically, the first step or steps), or may forget it all.

iii) Place-keeping errors
In activities with complex structures involving a number of different actions or mental processes to be performed in a particular sequence, children with poor working memory often lose track of what they have done and what has yet to be completed. Place-keeping errors can

lead to repetition of an element of the task such as counting an object more than once or writing a word down twice successively, or skipping a chunk of the task (for example, failing to count an object, or omitting one or more words in a sentence the child intends to write).

iv) Task abandonment

One of the most common consequences of working memory failure is that the child gives up a task completely, often after one of the kinds of error described in 1.i, 1.ii and 1.iii. In most cases, the task is abandoned because the child can no longer remember the information needed to guide an activity and, as a result, attention moves away from the task in hand. This loss of focus is a very distinctive hallmark of working memory failures, and has been termed 'zoning out'. This behaviour may fall 'below the radar' of teaching staff, particularly if the child is prepared to sit quietly waiting for the next activity to be introduced or for a prompt to be delivered that will enable him or her to process. On other occasions, low memory children may distract other pupils by engaging them in unrelated discussions or activities when they are no longer able to stay on task as a consequence of working memory failure.

2 Monitor the child

In order to provide effective support for children with poor working memory, it is recommended that teachers (and other individuals responsible for guiding the child through an activity) regularly monitor the child during mentally demanding activities. There are two main ways in which this can be effectively achieved, as described below.

i) Look out for the warning signs of working memory overload (see 1)

Signs of overload are incomplete recall, failing to following instructions, place-keeping errors and task abandonment. Because working memory failures often lead to inactivity, the child will need regular active monitoring, as the signs of failures may not be sufficiently salient to attract the attention of a busy teacher.

ii) Ask the child

One valuable strategy is to ask the child what he or she is doing, and what he or she intends to do next. Like adults, children are acutely aware of their working memory failures, and even from a young age are able to report accurately what they can remember and whether or not crucial information has been forgotten. They therefore respond well to prompts such as 'What are you going to write?', 'Who did I say you will be working with?' and 'Tell me what you have to do.'

This kind of monitoring is a fast and effective way of checking whether or not the child's working memory is overloaded. A further advantage of direct enquiry is that the act of repeating important information (rehearsal) can itself prolong storage of information in working memory, as discussed in Chapter 1.

There are several ways in which information can be re-supplied to the child. The instructor or a fellow pupil acting as a memory guide can repeat it (see 5), or the child can be directed to use any memory aids that are available to support the ongoing activity (see 6). Memory failures can also present a useful opportunity for explaining to the child the benefits of adopting memory-supporting strategies, and of providing guidance about how to use them proactively in the future to prevent memory loss (see 7).

3 Evaluate the working demands of learning activities

If the working memory intervention is to be effective, the teacher should be able to identify what, if any, features of a particular activity place significant demands on working memory. Once these have been identified, the activity can be modified to reduce working memory load (see 4) and so to increase the chances of successful completion. Here are some of the factors that influence working memory.

i) Excessive length

Because working memory is limited in capacity, lengthy sequences that exceed a child's capacity will not be remembered. As a rule of thumb, children with poor working memory under the age of ten years are likely to struggle to store sequences of three or more items that are unrelated, such as the number sequence *5, 9, 2* or a word list such as *cat, floor, car*. The longer the sequence, the greater the working memory demands will be.

ii) Content that is unfamiliar and not meaningful

In the two examples in i) above, there is no pattern underlying the sequence, or meaningful associations between the items. Low meaningfulness and high unpredictability place heavy demands on working memory, because children are not able to use their existing knowledge (in other words, long-term memory) to support their performance; they are therefore forced to rely only on their working memory which may have a small capacity. Remembering *5, 9, 2* therefore imposes a greater working memory load than *2, 4, 6*, and the sequence *cat, floor, car* is harder to remember than *mum, dad, son* because in both cases there are no meaningful links or knowledge that the child can take advantage of in his or her attempt to remember. An even more difficult task would be to remember lists composed of made-up words such as *filb, wum, qwot* in which even the individual sound sequences composing the items are unfamiliar, so the child has no opportunity to use his or her knowledge of the meaning of words to forge links between the items in the sequence.

Children often need to remember instructions that consist of sequences of actions. Some of these sequences are relatively meaningful, in that one step follows from the preceding one, as in *Stop what you are doing. Your first job is to tidy your tables. The second job is to stand behind your chair.* In this case, the instruction is probably one that is part of a regular classroom routine, so it will be highly familiar to the child, already stored in long-term memory, and will therefore impose minimal working memory demands. Consider the following instruction, the properties of which are rather different: *Take a whiteboard then pass it on. Take a pen then pass the bag on. Put the pen on your board. Put the rubber on the board.* This instruction has less predictable content, and also involves four steps rather than three. It will therefore impose greater demands on working memory.

Although these instructions contain many more than three words, children with low working memory will often be able to follow them if they are appropriately structured along the lines described above. The reason for this is that sentences that are meaningful and grammatical contain a lot of information that can be remembered in chunks using our existing knowledge of the world. Some instructions may also be remembered in terms of actions rather than sequences of words. So, because the seven-word sentence, *Take a whiteboard and pass it on*, really consists of just a single action (with two elements), a child with poor working memory is likely to be able to remember it, although he or she may struggle to remember *cat, floor, car*.

Some sentences nonetheless impose greater loads on working memory than others. Sentences with simple grammatical constructions and highly predictable content such as *The cat sat on the mat and licked its white paw* place fewer demands on a child's limited working memory capacity than sentences of the same length containing more complex syntax and less familiar content such as *To blow up parliament, Guy Fawkes had 36 barrels of gunpowder*. Thus if the task was to write down the sentence, a child with poor working memory would be expected to have fewer difficulties in remembering the first than the second sentence.

iii) A demanding mental processing activity

The working memory capacity available to support storage in an ongoing activity is directly affected by whether or not the child is also engaged in another mental activity that demands attention. Having to perform a challenging mental activity at the same time as storing information – as, for example, in the course of mental arithmetic – reduces the working memory capacity available for storage. As a result, what appears to be a fairly trivial memory load when the task only involves storage may exceed the child's working memory capacity when combined with another processing activity.

4 Reduce working memory loads

To support learning in children with poor working memory, it is often necessary to modify a learning activity in order either to avoid working memory failure, or to reduce memory demands in a task that has already generated signs of working memory failure (see 1).

There are two main points at which changes may be introduced. The first is in lesson planning. A class activity may need to be modified for the low working memory children to prevent working memory overload. Secondly, tasks may need to be modified as they take place if the warning signs of working memory failure are present (see 1). If a warning sign has been detected, the teacher may wish to modify the task and present it again, either immediately or on another occasion. Repeating a task, either with or without modifications, can be particularly beneficial in helping the child to become familiar with the requirements of the activity and the mental and physical demands it places, and this familiarity can in itself ameliorate working memory loads to some degree. This strategy was used effectively by many teachers participating in the intervention study, illustrated by the following note from our observations.

> The learning activity for identified pupils is a simple game being played for the third day in a row to increase familiarity of the rules and sounds. Little explanation of the activity was required, and the pupils worked without distraction.

A crucial first step before attempting to reduce working memory loads is to identify what the desired learning outcome of the activity is, and to ensure that this is preserved following the modifications. For example, the target may be for the child to write a complete sentence. In this case, the content of the sentence to be written can be readily modified in a variety of ways (outlined below) to minimise the chances of working memory failure; reducing the length of the sentence is likely to be valuable here. Another desired learning outcome may be for the child to write a sentence using connectives such as *and* or *but*. In this case, using short sentences may not be possible, and other ways of minimising working memory load (such as using highly predictable content for the two clauses and simple grammatical constructions, possibly accompanied by spellings of tricky words that the child might like to use) will have to be adopted. This approach therefore does not require the teacher to compromise the targets for the child's progress. Instead, the target is preserved and non-essential elements of the task are modified to reduce the likelihood of working memory overload and consequent task failure. Some methods for modifying in this way are outlined below.

i) Reduce the amount of material

The sheer bulk of information to be remembered can often be reduced, for example by using shorter sentences or by cutting down on the number of steps in an instruction. Another strategy is to make the content of instructions more memorable by using actions to accompany the verbal content, as in the following example: 'I am going to give you two books – your literacy and your red developing writing book. [Teacher points to them.] Your plan is in this literacy book. [Teacher points.] You will write the story in your developing writing book.' The accompanying actions make the meaning of the instructions very clear to the child, who may also be able to remember the actions and objects if the verbal content of the instruction is lost from working memory.

ii) Increase the meaningfulness and familiarity of material

Information that corresponds to knowledge that has already been acquired by the child can be remembered in a variety of ways in addition to using working memory. So, the sentence *Lions have stripes and live in the jungle* can be easily remembered because it corresponds directly to information that is already stored in the child's semantic memory, and so prevents the child from needing to rely exclusively on his or her limited working memory capacity.

Another useful strategy is to review a topic before a child starts to work on a memory-demanding activity that draws on this material. This strategy, which is widely used in many classrooms, activates the child's knowledge of the information, increasing the likelihood that her or she will be able to use long-term memory to support the activity if working memory is overloaded. Here are some examples from our observation notes.

> The teacher starts maths lesson by reviewing material covered in a previous lesson: 'Yesterday, we started to think about taking away. What else do we call that?'

Children perform a writing activity that is based on a topic that the class is currently studying in science (plants), in order to increase familiarity with the vocabulary and meaning of the text.

iii) Simplify mental processing

The majority of learning activities in the classroom involve the child not only remembering information related to the task, but also engaging in some demanding mental processing. This might involve understanding a new concept, reading a word, attempting to spell an unfamiliar word, comparing the sound structures of two words, or making a mathematical calculation. In each case, the mental processing involved will reduce the availability of working memory storage space. The working memory demands of a task can therefore be reduced by making the processing element less demanding.

One way of reducing processing demands in tasks that involve language information, as the majority of classroom-based activities do, is to simplify the grammatical structure of sentences. Complex sentence structure such as those containing embedded clauses (for example, *The boy that was carried by the girl had red hair*) and unusual structures (for example, *The horse raced past the barn fell*) place far greater demands on working memory than simple constructions. This is because it is difficult to understand the sentences at the same pace at which the words are spoken, so that the child (and adult) needs to rely on the stored form of the sentence in working memory to help them interpret the meaning. The delay in comprehension and in subsequent action will allow an already limited working memory capacity to decay further, leading to loss of crucial information. A low working memory child would therefore find it far easier to understand and remember the modified forms of these sentences: *The girl carried the boy with red hair* and *The horse fell as it raced past the barn*. Similarly, the sentence *To blow up parliament, Guy Fawkes had 36 barrels of gunpowder* could be usefully re-phrased as *Guy Fawkes had 36 barrels of gunpowder to blow up parliament*. This sentence structure is simpler and will be easier for a young child to remember.

The value of using simple grammatical forms is not restricted to sentence writing activities. Low working memory children will also benefit from receiving instructions that are simply presented. This applies both to general classroom management instructions and also to the detailed content of a learning activity. Consider, for example, the following mathematical reasoning problem given to a small group of seven-year-old children: *After Jill has eaten three of his sweets, John has only five left. How many sweets did John have to start with?* The two sentences are quite difficult for a young child to process because the question occurs after the crucial information has been presented. The *after* construction may also pose challenges for young children, particularly when located at the beginning of a sentence, as in this example. The working memory demands of the activity would be reduced if the instructions were re-phrased in the following way: *How many sweets did John have to start with? Jill ate three of them, and he has five left.*

There are many other opportunities to simplify processing including tapping a skill developed at an earlier stage in a particular subject area. In maths, for example, it is easier for a child to complete an addition sum successfully if it does not require carrying a ten unit. And in a phonics activity involving making comparisons of the sound structures of a pair of words, the child will find it less demanding to judge whether a pair of words rhyme (in other words, share both a vowel and following consonant) than if they share the final consonant only. In situations in which the child is failing at an activity due to excessive working memory loads, reducing processing difficulty along these lines will increase the child's chances of completing it successfully.

iv) Restructure complex tasks

Getting lost in the structure of a complex task is a frequent occurrence for children with low working memory, causing errors such as skipping and repeating information (see 1.iii). A number of strategies can be useful to help children avoid these place-keeping failures. In some activities, it is appropriate to break down multi-step tasks into separate independent steps, requiring the child to complete each step before providing the necessary information to guide him or her in the next step. Here is an example of this strategy. Note that the pupils here also benefited from other strategies, including prompting (see 2.ii).

In order to reduce the storage demands of the task, these instructions were written as numbered points on the worksheet. Certain pupils were also asked to repeat the instructions to the class by answering prompted questions such as 'What are you going to do first? What's next?' When asked to repeat one of the steps for completing the task, Sophie (an 11-year-old child with poor working memory) was unable to do so. However, when prompted by the teacher to refer to step 3 on the worksheet, Sophie soon regained her place. The teacher also suggested that the children first completed any that they are familiar with and Sophie successfully followed this advice, starting with the months of the year and days of the week before attempting those that she was less familiar with. In addition to modelling what was required of the students for this activity, the teacher also prompted the children to make sure that they understood the task. By starting with familiar items first, the teacher increased the difficulty level of the processing loads incrementally.

Some learning activities cannot readily be broken down into a sequence of independent steps. If this is the case, it can be very useful to find a means for the child to represent the different sub-activities and plot his or her progress through them using external aids. For example, the teacher may be able to work with the child in depicting the key elements of the task in diagrammatic form, possibly with the different elements distinguished by colour or some other visual cue. The child can then track his or her progress through the different steps in the task, marking each step off on completion. Other media described in sections 6 and 7 below are also valuable for representing both the structure and content of complex tasks.

Another strategy is for child's instructor to guide him or her through the task by using prompts. In an example of this practice from our intervention study, the teacher asked a child the following questions while he was struggling to write a sentence: 'What is the next word?', 'Think of a sentence using this word', 'What is the spelling pattern?' Here is a similar example, from a different teacher and pupil: 'What sentence are you going to write?', 'Which word is missing to complete your sentence?' This approach is particularly useful in improving the child's attentional focus on the task in hand, allowing the individual supporting the child to continuously monitor the child for working memory failures and to supply forgotten information when required. It is, however, highly demanding of the teacher's time and attention, and is only feasible when working either with individuals or with a small group of children. This level of support can yield substantial dividends, as the following note from our observations demonstrates.

> Pupil sits near the teaching assistant during the carpet session and is closely monitored and supported by her and the teacher. No problems were observed.

5 Be prepared to repeat

Children with working memory problems benefit greatly from judicious repetition of information to guide their ongoing activities: this information might relate to general classroom management instructions, to task-specific instructions, or to the detailed content intrinsic to an activity.

Because not all of the children in a class or group have the same needs for repetition, it is necessary to employ strategies that tailor repetition opportunities to the needs of the individual child. One valuable approach is to encourage them to request repetition when necessary. Children with poor working memory are often reluctant to make such requests, possibly because teachers may have indicated on previous occasions that they have failed to listen in the first place. To overcome this reticence, it is important to praise the child when seeking appropriate help in this way.

It can also be useful to partner a child with poor working memory with another pupil who has good memory abilities, and so can guide them through an activity with occasional prompts when requested. Although it is clearly important that this does not impose an undue burden on the more capable pupil, many able children respond well to being given this kind of responsibility and this kind of partnership has been used to good effect in several of the classrooms that have used the working memory intervention. If this approach is adopted, it is important to acknowledge the value of the 'memory guide' and to provide rewards for his or her assistance in the form of praise and other encouragements.

6 Encourage the use of memory aids

Supplying memory aids to pupils with poor working memory is a key element of the approach recommended here. Under the right conditions, the child is likely to benefit from external devices that either directly provide crucial information that can be lost from working memory, or that reduce the working memory demands.

Simply making memory aids available in the classroom is not sufficient to guarantee their use, and many children with poor working memory make little spontaneous use of aids. One factor influencing uptake and effective use of memory aids is physical proximity: children are much more likely to take advantage of devices that are within hand's reach than those that are physically distant, such as the board by the teacher's desk at the other end of the classroom. The reason for this is that the demands on attention are increased if the child has to shift from the task in hand to a distant rather than a close source of information. Because focused attention is crucial to maintain the contents of working memory, memory aids that place high demands on the child's attention can themselves cause the loss of the contents of working memory. Often, the children do not even try to attempt using memory aids that are distant, possibly as a natural strategy for conserving their attention for the current task.

Use of more distant memory aids can be encouraged by ensuring that children are highly familiar with their location and content. In one classroom participating in the intervention project, posters of key information were displayed prominently in the classroom and, in relevant activities, the teacher frequently directed the children's attention to the appropriate poster ('Today we are learning about sentences, which is a class target. We know what a sentence needs – look at the chart over here.'). This kind of familiarisation will promote ease of use of memory aids in all children in the class, and may be particularly beneficial to low ability children.

A second factor influencing the use of memory aids is the child's expertise at using them. As discussed above, children with poor working memory often do not use memory aids spontaneously, possibly because of the cost of transferring attention to the device: they find it demanding to engage with a memory aid in addition to juggling the processing and storage demands of a particular activity. One way to encourage the use of memory aids is to provide extensive practice in the use of memory aids in situations that place minimal demands on working memory. This training works particularly well for devices such as number lines, the use of which can become automatic with sufficient practice. Once the child has become skilled in using a particular aid so that it can be used relatively automatically (and hence requiring little diversion of attention), its application can be extended to situations in which the working memory demands are greater. In the intervention project, many teachers were observed to use this strategy effectively, regularly demonstrating how to use aids such as individual target cards, reading journals, spelling journals and number lines.

Here are some of the memory aids that are widely available in classrooms, and that can be used both to help prevent working memory failures and to aid recovery from them when they do occur.

i) Writing aids

As many of the examples in this book demonstrate, writing imposes substantial demands on working memory: the child has to hold in mind the intended message while attempting to write individual words, either from their knowledge of how the particular words are spelled or by applying the rules they have learned that map sounds onto letters. Difficulties in spelling one particular word in a sentence can therefore lead to working memory overload and complete loss of the information needed to guide the task through to completion. Providing the child with written spellings for words that he or she is likely to use is therefore extremely valuable in preventing working memory failures. Spelling aids include wall charts, spellings written on the class board, flash cards placed in view of the child, word strips, word blocks and personalised dictionaries within hand's reach of the child. For example, a *What is a sentence?* poster listing the key elements of a sentence can help guide the child's formulation of the content of the text to be written.

ii) Mathematical aids

Mathematics places heavy demands on working memory for children at all stages of their education, which is the reason why the majority of children with poor working memory struggle to make reasonable progress in this area of the curriculum. In the very early school years, children need to establish counting skills and basic number concepts; more often than not, a particular learning activity designed to promote this kind of learning will involve the child both storing number information and applying his or her developing conceptual knowledge and skills at the same time. At this stage, children are greatly helped by easily handled three-dimensional objects that can be readily counted such as cubes, beads and counters, and devices such as abaci and Unifix blocks.

Number lines are also valuable in supporting the working memory demands of simple mathematical operations such as addition and subtraction, as they provide an external record of the number that the child has reached in the calculation. Fingers are useful, too! Low working memory children typically rely more on the use of fingers to count than on other devices such as number lines that involve greater demands on their attention.

In older children, the working memory demands of mathematics remain significant. Learning activities may involve understanding and memorising mathematical rules such as multiplication rules. Still later, the child needs to learn and retrieve facts in the form of mathematical formulae (for example, relating to the calculation of area, volume and circumference) and apply these to the content of the problem on which he or she is working. In each case, devices supplying information that the child cannot readily retrieve from long-term memory will help greatly. There are many forms in which these memory aids come, including multiplication grids, other kinds of look-up devices, and calculators. The specific memory needs of the individual can also be addressed more directly by making available memory cards that supply information that the child is likely to need, to be re-used many times to promote familiarity.

iii) Audio devices

Although the majority of memory aids in use in the classroom are visual in nature, some schools also make excellent use of audio recording devices. The technology of these devices has improved greatly over recent years, and they can provide a valuable back-up for verbal material such as lists of instructions and more detailed content of learning activities. Moreover, because children as young as three years of age in nursery education are using these devices in play, they are often already highly skilled in their use.

iv) Computer software

Information technology such as educational computer programs, interactive whiteboards and digital notepads provide many opportunities for children to generate prompts for themselves by a variety of means including pointing and clicking on icons that supply useful information. Providing children with poor working memory with access to these flexible devices and the necessary training in their technical operation and their practical use in the classroom is extremely valuable.

We end this section with a description by a teacher who implemented the intervention approach in her own classroom, combining her own innovations with use of many of the strategies and principles discussed in this section.

> What I've found is that the children actually find it difficult to use memory aids when they are displayed on the wall or further away from them. They seem to lose the information between looking up at the display and returning attention to their work. We've made some small memory cards for each child that have general information for numeracy and literacy. So, there might be just one strategy for addition and subtraction that they can always refer to when we're doing that. Each child has their own memory cards on a keyring with information they might need in these subjects and we keep adding to them as we go along. They might have a list of connectives for literacy or useful maths vocabulary and they are there next to them, so they can use them when necessary. But for more specific information, like when I'm teaching fractions, I prepare an enlarged memory card for all of the children.

7 Develop the child's use of strategies for supporting memory

So far, the focus has been on strategies that the teacher can adopt to minimise the opportunities for working memory overload in low memory children. It is recommended that these teacher-led methods of support are supplemented by developing the children's own use of strategies that allow them to prevent or overcome memory problems. Arming the child with self-help strategies will promote their development as independent learners able to identify and support their own learning needs.

Some of the strategies that can be developed and used to good effect in the classroom by children with poor working memory are described below. In each case, successful use of the strategy will depend on training, practice and continued support from the teacher and, whenever possible, the child should be praised for using the strategies. It should be recognised that not all methods work equally well for all individuals, although it is always worth trying out a strategy that is of potential value and evaluating the extent to which the child finds it useful.

The extent to which children can take advantage of particular strategies will depend on their cognitive abilities, and particularly on working memory. Chapter 2 described how working memory profiles are often uneven, with a child having relative strengths and weaknesses across different areas. For example, many children with attentional deficits have weak verbal working memory and visuo-spatial working memory capacities but reasonably strong verbal short-term memory. Other children have relative strengths in either verbal working memory or visuo-spatial working memory.

Being aware of a child's working memory profile is useful as it allows the teacher to target the strategies that are likely to work well (see Chapter 2 for how to assess working memory). In general, children respond best to those strategies that capitalise on any working memory strengths, and also to those that compensate in a direct way for their working memory weaknesses. Children who have greater impairments in verbal than visuo-spatial working memory are therefore likely to be particularly effective at applying strategies that exploit non-verbal methods for remembering important information. This might include using long-term memory in a variety of ways (see 7.iv), and the use of diagrams and flow charts to help keep track of progress within a task. These children will also benefit from using devices that directly reduce their dependence on verbal working memory, such as audio recording devices (see 6.iv) and writing notes (see 7.iii). In contrast, children with relatively good verbal short-term memory skills would be expected to respond well to training in the use of rehearsal (see 7.ii), as this strategy operates directly on this component of working memory.

Some of the strategies that children with poor working memory can use to help themselves to prevent excessive working memory loads and to recover from memory overload when it occurs are outlined below.

i) Request help

One strategy that can easily be encouraged in children of all ages is to ask for help when important information has been forgotten, providing the opportunity to recover from working memory failures. The children are often reluctant to seek assistance in this way, and need encouragement to ask when necessary. The following observation from our intervention project records an example of effective support for this strategy.

> The teacher encourages pupils to ask for help when they are stuck or for information to be repeated when required. Ross attempted to develop this strategy at one point during the numeracy lesson when he voluntarily asked the teacher to explain the independent task to him again as he had forgotten the verbal instructions. Ross was praised for seeking help in this way.

It can be very useful for the teacher to discuss with the child the person who he or she should ask for assistance, in different situations: this may include the teacher, classroom assistants or other children (including, for example, a nominated memory guide, as discussed in 5). This will reduce the child's uncertainty about who to ask, and may minimise the disruptive effect of the request on the smooth running of the classroom.

ii) Rehearsal

Another relatively simple strategy that can be beneficial for the child is to rehearse verbal information that only has to be remembered for a brief period of time. Rehearsal consists of repeating a limited amount of verbal material, either silently or aloud (either works equally well). It is useful because it can prolong the content of verbal short-term memory, provided that the amount of information being rehearsed is not too great. However, rehearsal requires full attention: the consequences of distraction from either our own thoughts or from an interruption by someone else are disastrous when, for example, we are trying to keep in mind an unfamiliar telephone number while looking for a pen. This strategy is therefore most useful in situations with a significant short-term memory load but in which the child does not face any other mental processing demands that require attention. For example, rehearsal could be a very effective way of a child remembering a message that he or she has to deliver to a teacher in another classroom in the school. Telling the child to use rehearsal in this kind of situation – for example, by saying 'Saying the message over in your head until you see Mrs Jones will help you to remember it' – is likely to be very beneficial. Rehearsal will be less useful in situations in which the child has to remember the message while completing another activity, as in the following example: 'When Mr Pitkarji comes in after the mental maths session has finished, please remind him to leave his keys with Miss Blackburn'.

Explaining to the child the situations in which rehearsal is most useful – typically, ones in which storage is required and there is no other demanding mental activity – is recommended. It should be noted that as children do not typically start to use rehearsal spontaneously before seven or eight years, it is likely to be most effective as a strategy in older children.

iii) Note-taking

Children who have acquired basic literacy skills will benefit from using written notes to support their performance on complex or prolonged activities with several steps or stages. The children should be encouraged to write down for themselves important information needed to guide themselves through the activity, and also to check these notes regularly as the task is being performed to ensure that they are not making errors. Here are two excerpts from our observation notes recording teachers' support for this strategy.

> Encourages pupils to jot down important information to be remembered on their individual whiteboards when performing mental calculations.

> Tells pupils to list new words in their spelling journals and to note their own strategies for remembering them.

Younger children at the early stages of learning to read and write may benefit from a more rudimentary form of this strategy, in which they use symbols or their own invented spellings to form a list of the structure of a task to be completed. For example, consider an activity that we observed in a classroom in which five-year-old children were given a sheet containing ten flowers, and were asked by their teacher to colour-in the first, third and last flowers. A child with poor working memory made errors in this task because she was unable to remember the content (first, third, last) of the instruction. It would have been useful for the teacher to have asked the lower ability children in the classroom to write down the three numbers (1, 3, 10) before starting to colour-in the flowers. Note that at this young age, children are unable to use this kind of strategy spontaneously and will require explicit direction.

iv) Using long-term memory

One of the best ways to offset the demands placed on working memory by an activity is to encourage the child to rely on long-term memory where possible, by remembering material in terms of meaningful chunks rather than lengthy and arbitrary sequences of information. Effective use of long-term memory may involve some additional effort to help the child learn a particular chunking strategy, but the potential dividends are great. In one example in a school participating in the intervention project that we observed, nine- and ten-year-old children were being taught an acronym *CFSS* to help them remember the key properties of a sentence: 'always check for

Capital letters, Full stops, Spellings and Sense in sentences'. Because the acronym is short and had become highly familiar to the class through its repeated use, it will have become part of most children's long-term memory and will therefore not have imposed a working memory load on the children while completing their writing activities.

v) Place-keeping and organisational strategies

Because children with working memory problems typically experience marked difficulties in remembering how far they have progressed in complex tasks, encouraging them to break tasks down into their component parts and treat each part as a separate task to be completed before starting the next one can be very valuable. However, this strategy demands a high degree of awareness of the structure of a task (metacognition), and for this reason is not likely to be successfully employed in children below the age of eight years. Even older children will need to be encouraged to find ways of breaking down tasks, and may benefit in particular from training and regular practice in using visual devices such as diagrams and flowcharts to depict task structure. When organisational strategies are used, it is particularly important for the child to find a way of recording their progress to date in the task; this can help reduce the likelihood of the place-keeping errors that they frequently make.

Simpler strategies can be used with younger children to help them remember where they have got to in a task. One activity which lends itself particularly well to strategy support of this kind is counting, as illustrated in the following example from our observation notes.

Teacher shows pupils how to touch their chin as they count each finger so they remember which ones have been counted, and encourages them to use this strategy whenever counting. She also asks pupils to cross off the fingers on each picture as they count.

Because remembering the number they have counted up to can be challenging for children with poor working memory, these two strategies of recording in another modality their counting progress – either by touch or by making a mark visually – provide excellent means of supporting the working memory demands of the activity. The example below illustrates how a variety of strategies can go a long way towards compensating for the learning difficulties experienced by children with poor working memory.

In numeracy lessons, Sarah has developed a number of strategies to support her learning. For example, she counted on her fingers, used rough paper to perform calculations, and often talked herself through the steps of each calculation rehearsing them aloud. As an older student, Sarah is not only able independently to apply the suggested memory aids and strategies but also to create her own strategies to support her learning. This allows her to be more autonomous in her learning, a critical skill as older children often have fewer memory aids in the classroom than younger children and are expected to be independent in their learning process. By developing her own memory strategies, Sarah is also able to manage efficiently the memory loads in activities and retain information for longer periods.

POINTS TO REMEMBER

- Children with poor working memory struggle to meet the working memory demands of many classroom activities, and this impairs their rate of learning, particularly in academic subjects such as reading and maths.
- For these children, we recommend an intervention that is designed to minimise task failures due to excessive working memory load. This intervention can be used alongside current methods of curriculum delivery.
- The principles of the intervention, which are based on research and theory from cognitive psychology but also correspond to current good practice, are as follows: be aware of the warning signs of working memory failure, monitor the child, evaluate working memory load if the warning signs are detected, reduce the working memory load if necessary, repeat important information, use memory aids and encourage the child to use strategies for supporting working memory.

CHAPTER 6

Putting the intervention into practice

Overview

This final chapter provides further information about the working memory intervention outlined in Chapter 5. Some of the ways in which the principles of the intervention have been effectively combined in practice are described. Feedback is reported from teachers who have implemented the intervention. A brief exercise provides the opportunity for readers to practise applying the principles of the intervention to particular classroom situations. Finally, answers are provided to questions that are frequently asked about the intervention approach, and about working memory more generally.

Introduction

Chapter 5 described a classroom-based approach designed to help children with poor working memory overcome the many difficulties that they face in structured learning activities. In this final chapter, we provide further information about the practicalities of the intervention that is designed to guide any readers who may be considering adopting this approach themselves. The purpose of the intervention is to enhance the children's opportunities to learn and make good academic progress, by preventing and compensating for working memory overload. There is no detailed blueprint for this approach. Rather, it consists of a set of principles and strategies that can be applied by the teacher to fit the needs of the child, within the broader context of the other pupils, the requirements of the curriculum for the age group, and the school. The principles are to:

- recognise working memory failures
- monitor the child for these failures
- evaluate working memory loads
- reduce working memory loads when necessary
- be prepared to repeat information
- encourage the use of memory aids
- develop the child's use of strategies to support memory.

When used in combination, these principles and the strategies that are associated with them generate a robust framework of memory support for the child that minimises the adverse impact of working memory failures and in doing so accelerates learning.

At this point, many readers may be thinking about particular pupils in their own class who fit the description of children with poor working memory provided in Chapter 4, and wondering whether it would be useful and feasible to adopt this approach with them. Others may be making plans for the next school year, and considering whether some of the learning difficulties experienced by their pupils in previous years could be prevented by identifying the individuals with poor working memory and then implementing the intervention with them.

If you are considering whether or not to adopt this approach, there will be many questions that you will wish to ask before deciding to go ahead. For example, you will want to know how to put together the principles effectively for a particular child in a particular situation. You may also want to know about the practicalities of how much extra work is involved both in lesson planning and during teaching, and of how to juggle the different memory needs of children in your class. This chapter addresses the practical issues raised by the intervention, and provides more information about the ways that it has been successfully implemented so far. Where possible, we use the experiences and reports of teachers who have used the intervention approach themselves to do this.

Putting it all together: combining principles and strategies

Two particular features distinguish the classrooms that have made the most effective use of the approach. One is a preparedness to modify learning activities in ways that reduce dependence on working memory, whilst maintaining realistic learning targets for the children. On some occasions, the actual content of the lesson can be differentiated for low memory children in advance, in the process of lesson planning. On other occasions, the same lesson materials can be used with the whole class, but presented and supported in ways that prevent working memory overload for the low memory children. When tasks are differentiated in these ways, it seems to be most effective to group the child or children with poor working memory with other pupils of low abilities.

Some examples of task differentiation for low memory children are provided in the following excerpts from our intervention observation notes. The examples reflect the diversity of ways in which the different needs of these children can be accommodated: either the details of the activity can be changed, or external support can be provided, or the goals of the task modified.

Working memory load of the independent task is kept to a minimum: pupils are expected to read two pages only, working with their reading partner; questions based on reading are written in the pupils' individual reading journals with key words highlighted and with the page numbers provided.

Pupils move to the computers to work in pairs and are instructed to log on, and then to open up the word processing program they will use to complete the task. Pupils with low working memory are given word cards to remind them of their passwords.

Low memory pupils are only expected to write one simple sentence for each word, whereas more able pupils are expected to complete more.

During the mental maths lesson, calculations are shown pictorially as additions of coins as well as written number sentences. Pupils with low working memory are encouraged to make use of the visual information to support their calculation attempts.

The learning activity is to plan a fairy tale. More able children are given a guide consisting of the main elements of a fairy tale (location, characters, outcome, and so on). The children with low working memory and other less able pupils are provided with a more detailed planning framework that provides several options for each element (for example, possible locations are palace, woods and cave), from which the child can choose. Once pupils have made their choice, they rewrite the planned notes into structured sentences.

A second feature of those teachers who are very effective in implementing the intervention is that they often combine the different principles within a single learning activity. By using a number of different ways to support working memory, the child is provided with a framework of memory support – sometimes termed 'scaffolding' – that can both prevent and compensate for failures of working memory. Here are two examples from our observation notes of how the different elements of the intervention approach can be drawn together to allow the child to recover from the warning signs of working memory failure, and to complete the learning activity with success. The text in italics explains how the features of the activity relate to key elements of the intervention.

Two groups worked on this written task, one guided by the teacher and the other by the teaching assistant, whilst the third group completed a practical activity. [*This is an example of task differentiation, discussed earlier in this section.*] Sadie's group worked closely with the teacher who helped them to think of sentences such as: 'Tom went to the beach. He went into the rock pool.' [*This enables the teacher both to monitor the children for warning signs of working memory overload, and also to reduce working memory loads as necessary by guiding the children to generate appropriate sentences.*] She modelled how to write any new words as she sounded them out [*provides external memory support*] but did expect the children to attempt to spell any high frequency words independently. [*In this way, the learning target for the activity was preserved.*] Sadie began to struggle at this point and lost her place in the task when she had to write 'to the' without support, successfully writing the first word but failing to remember the second one. [*This is an example of a working memory failure leading to place-keeping difficulties.*] The teacher repeated the sentence a few more times [*repeat when necessary*], and prompted Sadie to refer to the appropriate word card displayed in the classroom to help her write the word. [*Supports the use of memory aids.*] With the support of frequent repetition of crucial information and use of memory aids, Sadie regained her place in the task and successfully completed it.

In a maths lesson, Tammy was supported by the teacher [*provides opportunity to monitor for warning signs of working memory failures*] when completing the first two calculations ($1 + 2 = 3$, $2 + 2 = 4$) but was left to attempt the others independently. She soon lost track in the calculations [*an example of place-keeping difficulties arising from working memory failure*] and began to struggle with $3 + 2 = ?$. Because Tammy's working memory and progress in the activity had been closely monitored by the teacher, she was quickly supported to regain her place in the task. [*Effective use of monitoring and repetition of information.*] The teacher encouraged her to look for the pattern in the numbers to help her continue the calculations, pointing out that the first and last columns increase by one each time whilst the second column always stays the same. [*Helps the child maintain focused attention on the activity.*] Tammy coped well with this strategy and successfully completed all of the calculations.

At its best, a convergence of strategies used pre-emptively can prevent working memory failures occurring at all. We end this section with some high points from our observations of the working memory intervention, in which the observer did not observe any activity failures in either reading or maths for two children from different schools, despite both children having substantial working memory problems.

Pupil has little opportunity to make working memory failures as teaching strategies support her extremely well.

Pupil is working in a small group, working closely with the learning support assistant – all tasks are tailored to the needs of the pupils with very little writing required and small degree of difficulty to ensure working demands are reduced as much as possible.

Intervention practice

This section presents a short exercise that provides the reader with the opportunity to practise applying the principles of the working memory intervention to specific classroom situations. Box 6.1 describes four classroom situations that might be challenging for a child with poor working memory. Imagine that you have such a child in your class. In each case, identify as many ways as you can in which working memory overload and task failure could be prevented for this child. Then, read on for our own suggestions of some ways in which each situation could be adapted to meet the needs of the low memory child.

Box 6.1

The classroom situations described below might be challenging for a child with poor working memory. In each case, use the principles of the working memory intervention to identify ways of preventing working memory overload. Suggestions for ways in which each situation could be modified follow.

Activity 1
It is close to the end of the lesson, and many of the children still have not completed the maths worksheet activity in which they have to manipulate coloured counters. The materials have to be collected together and put away, and the worksheets must be returned to each child's maths folder in their drawer. How would you organise the class, including children with poor working memory, in such a way as to achieve this efficiently?

Activity 2
The purpose of today's literacy lesson is to develop the skills of seven- and eight-year-old children in writing sentences about their own family. What support would you offer to the child with poor working memory?

Activity 3
As part of the phonics programme for five-year-old children, the class is engaged in an activity that involves clapping to each syllable in a nursery rhyme and counting the number of claps. Each child takes a turn in clapping along to one rhyme. How would you support the child with poor working memory when his or her turn comes?

Activity 4
You are a teacher of a class of nine-year-old children. Some shared classroom materials held currently by Mrs Taylor, a teacher in an adjoining building, are needed urgently in your own classroom. How would you go about giving the responsibility for this errand to a child with poor working memory?

Activity 1

- Do not give one long instruction that includes each step. Instead, guide the children through the sequence step by step, waiting for the class to finish performing one step before giving the next. It may help for the teacher to demonstrate the actions.
- Where possible, use the same routine each day to reinforce learning. For example, it may be feasible to end every day with a worksheet activity, to always require children to place worksheets in the folder and to always place the folder in the child's drawer.
- If a child completes the first step but does not progress further (a working memory warning sign), repeat the necessary information for him or her.

Activity 2

- Plan the lesson in advance, and ask the children to bring in photographs of their family members and a piece of paper with their names written on it. Ensure that this material is placed on the child's desk when the writing activity commences. If possible, ask the child to read aloud each name and point to the corresponding photograph. The teacher can help the child with any names that he or she cannot read.
- It would be useful to ask the child to draw a picture that depicts the content of the sentence before starting to write, which can then be used as a memory aid.
- After giving general guidance to the class about the content of the sentences, discuss with the low memory child what he or she intends to write. If the intended sentence is likely to generate a heavy working memory load, modify it by, for example, shortening it, simplifying its grammatical structure and ensuring that its content is highly meaningful.
- If the child shows warning signs of working memory failure once the activity has started (such as starting to write and then not progressing further, and making place-keeping errors such as skipping or repeating words), ask what he or she is doing now. If the child has forgotten the content of the sentence, provide cues that might help the child to generate it again, and ask for the sentence to be

repeated in order to reinforce it. If this strategy fails, repeat the sentence to the child.

- Provide key words (*sister*, *brother*, etc.) that the child can use, preferably located close to him or her.
- Supply a card or direct the child to a prominent poster displaying 'sentence starters' or cue words that can help the child begin each sentence.
- If an audio recording device is in use in the classroom and the child is skilled at using it, encourage him or her to record the sentence so that it can be re-played if forgotten.
- Praise the child for using any of the strategies or memory aids, and for asking for help if appropriate.

Activity 3

- Ensure that the child's turn occurs towards the end, making the task familiar to him or her and allowing them the chance to learn from the other children.
- To begin with, divide the class into two groups. Ask one group to clap to each syllable in a nursery rhyme while the other counts the number of claps. Simplifying the task in this way will reduce the working memory load, and will provide familiarisation and practice in the key elements of the task that can then be combined by asking the children to do both things – clap and count – at once.
- Encourage the children to use their fingers to count each syllable. This is a natural strategy that provides an external record of what number they have reached in their counting so far.
- Partner the child with a more able pupil, and start the task with the other pupil doing the clapping, and the child counting the claps. Then reverse the roles, with the same rhyme. Finally, let the child complete both elements of the task together, counting his or her own claps.
- For this child, use a very short rhyme with a simple structure, or a single line repeatedly. This will reduce the working memory load and allow her to focus on detecting the syllable structure of the material.
- Praise the child for working hard.

Activity 4
- One strategy for younger children would be to send the child with another more able pupil. The responsibility for the task may develop their confidence, and the other child provides a backup in case of working memory failure.
- Give the child some guidance about how best to remember the information. For example, ask the child to rehearse it continuously until he or she reaches the destination, and to avoid distractions or conversations with others that will cause working memory failure.
- Reduce the working memory demands of the errand by sending the child with a note providing the detailed content of the message, which the child can read if the message is forgotten, or pass on to the teacher.
- Explain to the child what to do if he or she forgets: 'Come back and tell me'.

Teacher perspectives on the working memory intervention

In this section, the time and commitment that are involved in implementing the intervention are considered. To address these important issues, we asked a group of teachers and learning support assistants who had implemented the approach for approximately half a school year some questions about their experience of the intervention. In each case, the teachers had in their class one or more children who had been identified as having very poor working memory via routine screening towards the end of the previous school year. Here are their answers to our questions.

Have you noticed any differences in the children as a result of the intervention?
'Definitely. The children are more settled, and their motivation is better. They are now able to identify the part they don't understand. [Note from authors: these children are nine/ten years of age.] So if I'm teaching maths problems, they are able to say: "I understand that bit and that but, that third bit, I don't quite understand". And we've moved on from me providing the memory cards to the children at the

beginning to the children making colour coded notes in their books to remind them of what they've found difficult or struggled on. So, it's a case of training them to help themselves.'

'Their self esteem has improved as well because they're not failing any more. They are now actually succeeding so self-confidence has hugely improved.'

'I find, especially with the ones that struggle more, that they're quite excited when they remember what they've got to do and when they're working they seem to be enjoying it a lot more.'

Were there any other benefits of taking part in the intervention?
'I am now aware of working memory as a special need and feel increasingly aware of these pupils and the strategies needed to support them. I can now identify pupils with working memory problems myself.'

'I know now that it's vital to develop set routines and structure in lessons and throughout the day to enhance my teaching and support these children.'

'I understand how important it is to repeat information and explain things again and again to these pupils to support them. You can't simply provide information once and move straight on or expect children to have taken it on board.'

'I use the strategies myself to help improve my own working memory. For example, as the Deputy Head, members of staff come and talk to me in the morning, and I'll have put my papers or car keys down somewhere. Then I'll go on to do something else and can't remember where I put those things when I need them. I've now learnt to organise myself and have routines of putting things in certain places so it doesn't matter if I'm distracted.'

Do you think that your colleagues have benefited from you taking part?
'One of the things about identifying working memory is it may change the psychology of how some teachers see this from a position of a child who is not engaged and has to learn to pay attention, to a child who perhaps has a complex special need. In which case,

teachers might feel it might motivate them to make more effort. What's happened as a result of this intervention is it is becoming recognised that this is not simply someone who can't be bothered, but is someone who has a complex difficulty which isn't always that apparent. Therefore, when you talk to colleagues who may not have as much understanding of working memory as you do, they may be less well disposed towards it partly because of the whole issue of culpability. We have to help people realise that though this is a child who could pay more attention, it's often as a result of difficulties beforehand.'

'Because of the tests you did on the children in my class where there were ten children identified as having working memory problems, my colleagues have empathy for me and we are already adjusting what we're expecting that class to achieve. We know that the next teachers will need to take on the strategies that I'm trying.'

What difficulties have you faced in implementing the intervention?
'One of the things I found difficult was using the repeating strategy when I was working in a small group. I put a lot of the children with working memory difficulties in a small group, which was a mistake. I would repeat a sentence to the first child, then the second and the third. But by the time I got to the third child, the first child was listening in to what I was saying to the third child and getting that mixture. So now I'm targeting the children over a week but keeping them in mixed ability groups which has helped.'

'To really get as much as possible out of the approach, it is necessary to put in lots of preparation time, particularly in modifying materials for the low working memory children and the other less able pupils. All the time I spent doing this paid off, but there is only so much time available in any one working day, and I often felt disappointed I couldn't do more when I knew what could have been achieved with extra preparation.'

Do you think that taking part in the working memory intervention will continue to influence your classroom approach once the study has finished?
'We have been discussing whether we need to consider more widely

all the other children in the school as well. It's become a way of teaching for us now more than anything, and we now need to disseminate it to all the other staff so it becomes part of their teaching. We're hoping to make this quality teaching and a school strategy.'

What further information would you have found useful in helping you to implement the intervention?
'I'm definitely going to take on what was said about the memory cards and keyrings [see Chapter 5, section 6]. I already used several tools and memory aids but those ideas are new to me. It would be good to have examples of memory aids.'

Would it help to provide parents/carers with more information about the approach?
'Yes. It goes back to the idea of parents telling them to go upstairs, brush your teeth, get changed, get your school kit, come back downstairs with your bag ... but he just doesn't do it. And that's the attitude parents come back with that he's just not listening to me. We need to help the parents understand that it's not that they're not listening.'

'It's something as simple as saying to them that the next time you send them upstairs, ask them how many things they have to do and to count up the number of things they need to do. This provides a routine if they can do it that way because we all know that, as a parent, we don't get strategies or packs of information. But we do it professionally because this is what we're taught and we understand it.'

'There's no reason why parents couldn't have the same information as teachers. With autistic children, we send home the visual timetable packs, but there are so many other children that would also benefit from the symbol to get dressed or get their bag. And if they just had that in the morning to look at rather than hold it all in mind when their parents tell them – you can't go back to speech, particularly if you have a poor working memory.'

'Children do a lot of their learning at home as well as at school, particularly if they have parents who are willing to help. Surely it makes sense to let the parents know too how to help the children, then we can all work in the same direction.'

Frequently asked questions

There are some questions that we are often asked about the impact of working memory on the classroom that have not so far been addressed in the book. Some of these questions relate to the intervention, and others concern other issues that impact on understanding how working memory relates to learning.

Do I have to change what I teach, and plan different learning activities for this child?
There is no need to change radically the way that you teach to use this approach effectively. You will be able to work with the current lesson content, although it will be necessary to make some modifications in order to prevent working memory overload. The principles and strategies that form the basis of the approach are simply ways of ensuring that within regular classroom activities, the child is not placed in situations where he or she is not able to remember what they are doing. Modifying lesson activities for low memory children is also a highly effective way of preventing working memory failures, as discussed earlier in this chapter.

I have a child in my class who is making very slow progress, but as far as I know does not have a particular problem with working memory. Would there be any problem in trying out this intervention for him?
If this child is frequently failing during structured learning activities, it would definitely be worthwhile to apply the principles of the intervention and finding out whether his performance improves when working memory loads are reduced. This approach will not harm anyone, and you will be able to judge for yourself whether you are seeing any improvements and so whether it is worth continuing. If you want to investigate more systematically whether this child does have a working memory problem, you might consider using the Auto-

mated Working Memory Assessment to assess his working memory strengths and weaknesses (see Chapter 2 for more information). The short screening version of this computer-based test only takes about ten minutes to administer.

I already incorporate most of the intervention strategies in my teaching. Is it really anything new?

This approach does indeed draw on many existing elements of good teaching practice, and many teachers apply these principles and strategies instinctively. By combining these methods in a focused and consistent manner, the child will be able to draw upon a framework of memory support that will prevent or compensate for working memory failures and this substantially increases the opportunities for learning.

I have a new class starting in a couple of months' time, and I'm interested in using this approach to prevent learning difficulties developing for individual children over the coming year. What should I do to start?

There are two possibilities. The first is to identify at the beginning of the year any children in your class who have working memory problems. This can easily be achieved by screening the whole class using the Automated Working Memory Assessment (see Chapter 2 for more details). This will take about ten minutes per child and does not require any specialist training. Test scores are automatically generated by the computer software and identify any areas of significant working memory problems. The intervention approach can then be directed to any children identified in this way with poor working memory.

The second option is to use the children's own behaviour to identify those individuals who may have working memory problems. Characteristics of children with poor working memory problems are described in Chapter 4 and their classroom learning difficulties, including signs of working memory failures, are outlined in Chapter 5. Any children who fit these behaviour profiles and who are making slow progress in learning are likely to benefit from the intervention.

I've used the Automated Working Memory Assessment to screen all of the children in my class. One boy scored at a very low level, but is making perfectly good progress in all areas. Why is this?

The first step we recommend in this situation is to check the child's working memory again on a couple of the tests of which he or she scored poorly before. The child may simply have been having a bad day when he completed the original assessments, and if performance moves into the average range on the second occasion, think no further of it. If, on the other hand, the memory scores remain low on re-test, you can be confident this child really does have poor working memory. In this case, his reasonable levels of academic attainments are probably due to other areas of significant cognitive strengths that provide opportunities to compensate for weaknesses in working memory. However, poor working memory presents a significant academic risk and the child may well start to struggle at a later point. Therefore although no active intervention is needed for this child, we do recommend keeping a watchful eye out for problems that may develop.

Is working memory affected by physical factors such as diet and exercise?

Like all cognitive abilities, working memory depends on the brain, and more specifically on the frontal areas of both the left and right hemispheres of the brain. As good diet and physical health are crucial for functioning of the brain as well as other organs of the body, working memory would be expected to function best in a healthy and well-nourished individual. However, there is no specific evidence of which we are aware that working memory problems are caused by poor diet or health, or that working memory capacity is directly boosted by dietary supplements in children who are already healthy.

Can stress, anxiety or other types of emotional problems cause poor working memory?

Although emotional disturbances are rarely the cause of the kind of persistent and unvarying working memory problems that we have described in this book, they can lead to more intermittent and temporary reductions in working memory capacity. Severe anxiety and depression are linked with impairments in concentration which will also affect working memory, and even mild symptoms of anxiety are associated with low levels of working memory performance. When a person is anxious, thoughts relating to the source of anxiety can dominate and take up valuable processing capacity, reducing the capacity that is available to store information in working memory. The impact of anxiety on performance of a particular task depends on the extent to which it requires working memory. Activities that place minimal demands on working memory will not suffer very much even if anxiety levels are high. However, if both anxiety levels and working memory loads are high, the child's performance will inevitably suffer. For this reason, emotional disturbances should be considered to be a potential cause of poor working memory function in children known to have mental health problems.

Can working memory be improved directly by training?
This is a very important question for which there is as yet no clear answer. We have no direct evidence that general working memory capacity can be improved by training in low memory children. Some research has attempted to enhance working memory by training children in the use of highly specific strategies, but the gains have been small despite intensive training, and have not generalised to other memory situations. However, an intensive computer-based training program has recently been developed boosts performance on working memory tests in children with ADHD (Attention Deficit Hyperactivity Disorder). The program is called Robomemo, and has been developed by CogMed in Stockholm. The training may work by improving children's abilities to maintain focused attention, or by developing their working memory capacities. We are planning a study to investigate whether children with poor working memory also benefit from participating in this training, but as yet we do not know the outcome. In the meantime, we strongly recommend an approach that seeks to avoid working memory failures in structured learning activities, as outlined in Chapter 5 and this chapter.

Do working memory problems persist beyond the early and middle childhood years?

Children with poor working memory usually do not grow out of the problem. Although the everyday manifestations of working memory problems remain significant at all ages through childhood and adulthood, they change considerably as people get older because cognitive demands and expectations differ. In education, older school children and adult students with poor working memory tend to struggle with the working memory demands of lecture-based presentations that require them simultaneously to understand new material and to take notes. They also often find it very difficult to maintain attention over lengthy study periods, and to synthesise and organise large amounts of material from different sources in a coherent fashion in preparing written work. On the positive side, older students are often (or at least the ones who are successful enough to enter tertiary education) more effective than younger children at using their own strategies to overcome working memory-related problems. In a recent survey of university students, we found that these strategies included taking frequent breaks during study, setting realistic targets for periods of work, reading lecture notes in advance of the lecture, and taking abbreviated and schematic rather than full notes. Students can also take advantage of IT facilities and other external memory aids such as digital audio recorders to overcome their memory problems. Individuals with poor working memory are often able to make educational and career choices that steer them away from learning and work situations that impose working memory loads that are, for them, excessive.

Does working memory capacity decline in older age?
Working memory capacity starts declining in middle age and continues to do so into older age, for most individuals. However, age-related loss in working memory is not very large, and can be compensated for well by knowledge and skills acquired earlier in life and by effective use of memory aids and strategies. Regularly engaging in cognitively demanding activities such as crosswords that require focused attention and access to stored knowledge is believed to be beneficial for cognitive function more generally.

> ## POINTS TO REMEMBER
>
> ■ Teachers who are particularly effective at implementing the intervention approach often do two things very well: they modify learning activities appropriately for children with low working memory, and are also successful at combining a number of principles and strategies in a single activity to provide a strong network of working memory support.
>
> ■ Feedback from teachers who have implemented the intervention approach indicate that there are substantial benefits for the child, the teacher and other school staff. It does, however, require considerable time and commitment for best results.

Concluding remarks

The aim of this book has been to explain what working memory is and the limits it places on children's classroom learning, in terms that are comprehensible to readers such as teachers who may not be familiar with the cognitive psychology of memory. The book describes our current understanding of how working memory impacts on a child's learning, based on research of our own team and that of many other groups across the world.

One limitation of this book is the impression that it gives that learning only takes place in the classroom. This is, of course, far from true. Parents, carers and the child's home environment provide a rich context for supporting learning both formally (for example, helping with homework) and informally, as a source of new information and the provider of opportunities for learning. The child is also an independent learner who is able to take advantage of the environment to reinforce and develop understanding of the world. Because as yet our own research has not moved into these areas of 'free-range' learning, we are regrettably not able to describe the ways that working memory limitations can impact on them. We aim to do so in the future, and in particular to provide support tailored for the many concerned parents and carers of children with working memory problems. In the meantime, it is hoped that the book will nonetheless be valuable to families as well as teachers who can use it to help understand why their children may struggle to learn.

In order to make the material in this book accessible to readers who do not have a background in academic psychology or education, a non-technical approach has been adopted in which detailed references to research studies have not been included. While we hope that this approach has made the book easy to read, it may have the less fortunate consequence of under-playing the extent to which current understanding of working memory and its impact on learning is based on a substantial body of research that has accumulated over the past 20 years or so. Those who wish to find out more about the research that lies behind this book are directed to the bibliography following this chapter, which provides a list of the relevant research papers and other publications that may be of use in guiding further reading in this area.

Glossary

ADHD
Attention Disorder Hyperactivity Deficit. A clinical disorder associated with hyperactive/impulsive and inattentive behaviour.

Attainment level
With respect to National Curriculum tests, the level of performance reached by an individual child, expressed with reference to the national benchmarks of expected achievements for particular age groups.

Attention span
An individual's capacity to maintain focused attention in the course of an ongoing activity.

Autobiographical memory
The long-term memory system supporting memory for significant events across the lifetime.

AWMA
The Automated Working Memory Assessment, a computerised test battery that assesses an individual's capacity in each sub-component of working memory.

Backward digit recall
A measure of verbal working memory involving the recall of digit sequences in reverse order.

Centile point
The score obtained by a particular percentage of the population on a particular measure. For example, the 10th centile point is the score achieved by the lowest 10% of the population, and the 90th centile point is achieved by the top 10%.

Central executive
The sub-component of working memory that controls attention and coordinates activity both within the working memory system and between working memory and other cognitive systems such as long-term memory.

Chunking
The grouping together of individual items into an integrated whole to enhance recall, typically using long-term memory.

Code of Practice
The UK system of classifying the severity of a child's special educational needs (SEN).

Cognitive psychology
The academic discipline concerned with the processes involved in high-level mental activities such as memory, reasoning, language and thought.

Developmental disorder
A condition in which a child fails to develop in a typical manner, with or without a known cause.

Digit recall
A measure of short-term or working memory involving the presentation and recall of sequences of numbers.

Distractibility
The tendency to be distracted from an ongoing activity by task-irrelevant thoughts or events.

Episodic memory
The long-term memory system supporting memory for events in the relatively recent past, typically spanning minutes through to days.

Focused attention
The capacity to maintain attention at will in the course of an ongoing activity.

Forward digit recall
A measure of verbal short-term memory involving the recall of a sequence of digits.

Hyperactive/impulsive behaviour
Elevated levels of problem behaviours relating to excessive motor and vocal activity, associated with ADHD.

Inattentive behaviour
Elevated levels of problem behaviours relating to failures to maintain focused attention on an ongoing activity, associated with ADHD.

IQ
Intelligence Quotient. A measure of an individual's general mental abilities based on several tests of knowledge and cognitive skills, expressed with respect to typical levels for a particular age (a score of 100 is average).

Long-term memory
Memory for experiences that occurred at a point in time prior to the immediate past, and also for knowledge that has been acquired over long periods of time. Long-term memory systems include episodic memory, autobiographical memory, semantic memory and procedural memory.

Memory cards
Individualised memory prompts used in the classroom.

Memory guide
A child nominated to assist a fellow pupil with memory-related problems.

Memory span
A measure of the maximum amount of material that an individual can successfully remember on a test of working memory.

Mental arithmetic
Calculations that involve the retrieval of mathematical knowledge and possibly its application to particular problems that do not use external devices or memory aids.

Mental imagery
Sensory images that are generated and stored in memory. These are typically visual in nature, but less commonly can also be auditory (relating to sound) or tactile.

Mnemonist
An individual who has exceptional memory abilities, which are often used for professional purposes.

National Curriculum
The specification of the curriculum that must be taught from 5 to 16 years in state schools in the UK.

Performance IQ
The IQ sub-score that relates to abilities on IQ tests that do not involve language.

Primacy effect
The more accurate recall of items occurring at the beginning of a sequence than those appearing at subsequent positions.

Procedural memory
Long-term memory for skills such as cycling that have been acquired through repeated practice and that can be executed 'automatically', without mental effort.

Reading comprehension
Understanding of text that an individual has read.

Reading span
A measure of verbal working memory in which the individual reads a series of sentences, and then attempts to recall the final word of each sentence in order.

Recency effect
The more accurate recall of items occurring at the end of a sequence than those appearing at prior positions.

Rehearsal
The voluntary act of mentally repeating information, typically with the

aim of prolonging its storage in working memory. Rehearsal is a particularly important strategy associated with verbal short-term memory.

School Action
Classification indicating that a child requires assistance from an external specialist to meet his or her needs, as specified by the UK Code of Practice.

School Action Plus
Classification that a child requires additional or different support in school, as specified by the UK Code of Practice.

Semantic memory
The long-term memory system supporting knowledge such as facts and word meanings.

SEN
Special Educational Needs. In the UK, recognition of SEN is associated with the necessity of differential provision for the child in school.

STM
Short-term memory. The ability to hold information in mind for short periods of time.

Statement of special educational needs
Classification that a child requires additional resources to support learning, as specified by the UK Code of Practice.

Synaesthesia
The unusual natural ability of some individuals to remember verbal or conceptual information in terms of particular colours or other sensations.

Verbal
Relating to abilities or information that can be expressed in terms of language.

Verbal IQ
The IQ sub-score that relates to an individual's abilities on IQ tests involving verbal material.

Verbal short-term memory
The sub-component of working memory that stores verbal information.

Visuo-spatial
Relating to abilities or information that can be expressed in terms of physical characteristics relating to vision, space, or movement.

Visuo-spatial short-term memory
The sub-component of working memory that stores information relating to vision, space, or movement.

Working memory
The ability to hold and manipulate information in mind for brief periods of time in the course of ongoing mental activities, consisting of a system of three sub-components: verbal short-term memory, visuo-spatial short-term memory, and the central executive.

Working memory capacity
The limit on the amount of information that can be held in working memory. Each sub-component of working memory has its own limit.

Working memory profile
The particular strengths and weaknesses of an individual across the different sub-components of working memory.

Zoning out
Mind-wandering, particularly when an individual is engaged in demanding cognitive activities.

Bibliography

There is an extensive research literature on working memory in children that spans three decades and thousands of journal articles. The publications listed below provide further information about the identification of working memory problems in childhood and the learning difficulties that are associated with them.

The following books provide detailed accounts of a range of developmental conditions that are associated with poor working memory and learning difficulties.

Alloway, T.P. and Gathercole, S.E. (2006). *Working Memory in Neuro-developmental Conditions*. Psychology Press.

Pickering, S.J. and Phye, G. (2006). *Working Memory and Education*. Academic Press.

Methods of assessing working memory and the working memory profiles associated with several developmental disorders are also described in this review paper.

Gathercole, S.E. and Alloway, T.P. (2006). Short-term and working memory impairments in neurodevelopmental disorders: Diagnosis and remedial support. *Journal of Child Psychology and Psychiatry*, 47, 4–15.

Here is the full publication information for the two standardised working memory test batteries discussed in the book.

Alloway, T.P. (2007). *Automated Working Memory Assessment*. Harcourt Education: London.

Pickering, S.J. and Gathercole, S.E. (2001). *Working Memory Test Battery for Children*. Harcourt Education: London.

More detailed reports of research studies discussed in the book are provided in the following journal articles.

Alloway, T.P., Gathercole, S.E., Adams, A.M. and Willis, C.S. (2005). Working memory abilities in children with special educational needs. *Educational and Child Psychology*, 22, 56–67.

Alloway, T.P., Gathercole, S.E., Adams, A.M., Willis, C.S., Eaglen, R. and Lamont, E. (2005). Working memory and phonological awareness as predictors of progress towards early learning goals at school entry. *British Journal of Developmental Psychology*, 23, 417–26.

Gathercole, S.E. and Pickering, S.J. (2000). Assessment of working memory in six- and seven-year old children. *Journal of Educational Psychology*, 92, 377–90.

Gathercole, S.E. and Pickering, S.J. (2000). Working memory deficits in children with low achievements in the national curriculum at seven years of age. *British Journal of Educational Psychology*, 70, 177–94.

Gathercole, S.E. and Pickering, S.J. (2001). Working memory deficits in children with special educational needs. *British Journal of Special Education*, 28, 89–97.

Gathercole, S.E., Brown, L. and Pickering, S.J. (2003). Working memory assessments at school entry as longitudinal predictors of National Curriculum attainment levels. *Educational and Child Psychology*, 20, 109–22.

Gathercole, S.E., Pickering, S.J., Knight, C. and Stegmann, Z. (2004). Working memory skills and educational attainment: Evidence from National Curriculum assessments at 7 and 14 years of age. *Applied Cognitive Psychology*, 40, 1–16.

Gathercole, S.E., Alloway, T.P., Willis, C.S. and Adams, A.M. (2006). Working memory in children with reading disabilities. *Journal of Experimental Child Psychology*, 93, 265–81.

Jarvis, H.L. and Gathercole, S.E. (2003). Verbal and non-verbal working memory and achievements on national curriculum tests at 11 and 14 years of age. *Educational and Child Psychology*, 20, 123–40.

Kane, M.J., Brown, L.H., McVay, J.C., Silvia, P.J., Myius-Gameys, I. and Kwapil, T.R. (2007). For whom the mind wanders, and when – An experience-sampling study of working memory and executive control in daily life. *Psychological Science*, 18, 614–21.

Pickering, S.J. and Gathercole, S.E. (2004). Distinctive working memory profiles in children with special educational needs. *Educational Psychology*, 24, 393–408.

Index

Learning Styles and Inclusion

Gavin Reid, **University of Edinburgh**

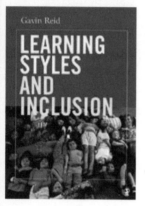

`In this book, Gavin Reid has grasped the nettle (of inclusion) with both hands and provided a text that is full of common sense and practical suggestions as to how the mainstream teacher can draw upon recent psychological theory and research to enhance the learning of all children. He jumps on no bandwagons but draws judiciously from a wide range of approaches to assessing learning styles and links what can be learned about groups and individuals from such techniques to helpful classroom practice' - *Professor Bob Burden, School of Education and Lifelong Learning, University of Exeter*

Drawing on his considerable experience as a teacher, educational psychologist, lecturer and author, Gavin Reid illustrates how to assess pupils' different learning styles and how to vary your teaching style to appeal to all types of learners, including disaffected students and those with special educational needs.

This book provides an overview of the different stages in the learning cycle; describes the differences between learners; and emphasizes the role the classroom environment and different teaching styles play in children's ability to learn. Readers will see how an understanding of learning styles can be used to encourage and promote good inclusive practice.

Ideas for assessment of learning styles and examples of different teaching styles will prove invaluable to class teachers, trainee teachers, SENCOs, LEA advisers; NQTs and NQT advisers and school management.

Contents
Learning Models and the Learning Cycle / Learning Differences and Learning Styles / The Role of the Learning Environment / Background to Learning Styles / Assessment of Learning Styles / Learning Styles / Learning and Teaching / The Inclusive School / Characteristics and Challenges / Learning Styles in the Inclusive Context / Promoting Effective Learning / Learning Styles / Strategies and Insights

September 2005 • 192 pages
Hardcover (978-1-4129-1063-7) Price £60.00 • Paperback (978-1-4129-1064-4) Price £18.99